Screenplay

Tips and Tricks for Writing and Revising Screenplays

(The Authoritative Guide for Converting Your Script Into a Novel)

Milton Hewitt

Published By **Chris David**

Milton Hewitt

All Rights Reserved

Screenplay: Tips and Tricks for Writing and Revising Screenplays (The Authoritative Guide for Converting Your Script Into a Novel)

ISBN 978-1-77485-487-7

No part of this guidebook shall be reproduced in any form without permission in writing from the publisher except in the case of brief quotations embodied in critical articles or reviews.

Legal & Disclaimer

The information contained in this ebook is not designed to replace or take the place of any form of medicine or professional medical advice. The information in this ebook has been provided for educational & entertainment purposes only.

The information contained in this book has been compiled from sources deemed reliable, and it is accurate to the best of the Author's knowledge; however, the Author cannot guarantee its accuracy and validity and cannot be held liable for any errors or omissions. Changes are periodically made to this book. You must consult your doctor or get professional medical advice before using any of the suggested remedies, techniques, or information in this book.

Upon using the information contained in this book, you agree to hold harmless the Author from and against any damages, costs, and expenses, including any legal fees potentially resulting from the application of any of the information provided by this guide. This disclaimer applies to any damages or injury caused by the use and application, whether directly or indirectly, of any advice or information presented, whether for breach of contract, tort, negligence, personal injury, criminal intent, or under any other cause of action.

You agree to accept all risks of using the information presented inside this book. You need to consult a professional medical practitioner in order to ensure you are both able and healthy enough to participate in this program.

TABLE OF CONTENTS

INTRODUCTION	1
CHAPTER 1: WRITE YOUR OUTLINE FIRST.	5
CHAPTER 2: WHAT IS A LOGLINE?	9
CHAPTER 3: THE 3 ACT STRUCTURE	16
CHAPTER 4: THE MAIN CHARACTER	24
CHAPTER 5: THE OPPOSITION	31
CHAPTER 6: THE SUPPORTING CAST	39
CHAPTER 7: LOVE INTEREST	48
CHAPTER 8: ACCELERATING MOMENT	53
CHAPTER 9: EMOTIONAL DECISION	57
CHAPTER 10: THE MAIN CHARACTER'S GOAL	63
CHAPTER 11: GENRE	69
CHAPTER 12: THEME	76
CHAPTER 13: EXAMINING YOUR BOOK'S POTENTIAL AS A FILM OR SERIES	83
CHAPTER 14: EXAMPLE OF PERFORMING AN BOOK TO FILM ASSESSMENT	106
CONCLUSION	180

Introduction

Many of the most popular films started as books, which includes the studio-produced and independent films. A few documentaries as well as films or TV shows are also based or made from books. Some of the major movies that began as books include The Harry Potter series, The Lord of the Rings, One Flew Over the Cuckoo's Nest, A Game of Thrones, The Hunger Games, The Joy Luck Club and many more.

On the other hand certain films were scripted but were later published as books or developed into series. In other instances news stories were made into films or books or both. Therefore, there are numerous paths to success in the field of film.

So , how do you transform your own script or book into a film series? While the process is intense, you can improve your odds of success by knowing the process. Transform your Book (or Script into a Film was designed to teach you how.

The book is based upon my experience of writing and producing more than a dozen documentaries, films and TV/film series the majority of which are in distribution with different distributors, others are in post-production or scheduled to be filmed in the coming six months. I have also written book-to-film critiques and looking over scripts on behalf of dozens of clients because of my work with various book publishing and promotion firms and also clients who found me through the Internet. I've also been writing treatment scripts and treatments that are inspired by non-fiction and fiction books that clients have requested and also creating promotional sizzle reels that make the book or script make an impact.

In this book the three primary methods to have your story or script transformed into a movie.

- You can sell the rights to the film to the book production or producer company, often with the assistance from an agent. In this instance it is usually necessary to already be famous or have millions of followers or have the book which has been the top seller. If you don't, agents and producers generally require the synopsis and the an outline for the stand-alone feature or an Show Bible with a sample script for a show. It's also beneficial to include a sizzle reel, another term for a script or book trailer in order to attract attention to your work.

You can create your own film independently to accelerate the process of turning your book into a film and then find an agent. In this scenario you'll need only the script. There's you don't need an agent's letter of inquiry, Show Bible, or sizzle reel. This could help you create the treatment or have it made by you. It is basically a outline of the most important elements or plot points of the book that can guide you on the best scenes you want to incorporate into your film or in an episode of the form of a series. When you've decided to produce the film yourself, you'll have to locate or create an production team, or engage a director or producer to create the team. In addition, you must get the funding, typically through your own resources or family members and friends when you are making your first time making a film. In general, you will need all of the funds in advance to pay for the production.

Good luck when you decide to turn your book and/or script into movie using this book.

Chapter 1: Write Your Outline First.

An outline can also be referred to as "beat sheet" or "beat sheet" in the field It has been proven to be beneficial before writers start the long work of starting their script. An outline before hand will keep the writer from working in circles. Personally, I find it more efficient to start working on characters first, then my outline, then my script. Then I start to realize that the story is beginning to develop and coming to life.

2. When writers are just starting out, commit the error of altering the fundamental ideas during the initial draft, before even completing it.

The reason is that they find out that the story's origin story requires significant tweaks, but in reality, they haven't even had the chance to see it come to life. However, I must inform that you now, prior to deciding to make any changes, you must finish your first draft. You should work on one idea until the very end until you are able to alter the idea. If you are constantly putting off and trying to avoid the final outcome by making changes repeatedly it isn't being productive, but you are simply sustaining the pattern of never working on any task. Don't get too hard on yourself. We've had to write terrible drafts in the beginning. But, keep in mind you're the sole way to achieve the perfect the tenth draft is by creating your first draft.

3. Explore as many screenplays as you can and this will act as your source of ideas. Explore the greatest minds in cinema, from old masters to the contemporary brilliant minds. There's no reason to not having access to screenplays since they are available on the Internet can be a gold trove of scripts to help you along the path. Learn about scripts from the genre you'd like write for.

4. Gather a group of friends who enjoy writing.

Screenwriters who have an support group is among the most beneficial ways to progress forward on your path. I suggest meeting every week at least once for constructive critiques of the scripts of others. It isn't easy finding readers which is why having a group of writers is a good alternative. They will be able to spot certain aspects of your script which you might not have thought of at the beginning. Their feedback will give you a great idea of the story. You'll be able to tell whether your joke is successful and if others are able to see it. The group should be supportive at the heart; it's not intended to be a community in which you have to slam the work of others and then make a big deal of the negative remarks around. Find the positive aspects of the work and tell the truth about your opinion of an article.

5. Screenwriting can be a real pain.

If you'd like to be successful in this field, be aware of this fact as the best it is. Certain people keep writing forever.

6. Just keep going.

Honest, consistent, and hard work is going to lead you to the opportunities will help you begin the career path you want to take in Hollywood. Don't judge other people you encounter in the process, based on their methods or choices to do things. We're all here together and enduring similar struggles.

The process of creating your first screenplay or any screenplay, for that matter, is a long-term commitment. It's a marathon, much more than a race. Don't be intimidated by other people who produce the latest blockbuster within several weeks. Everyone has their own style and own process to take into consideration. In the end, just be sure to take your time and have fun doing it!

Chapter 2: What Is A Logline?

The logline is at the core and the essence of the screenplay. It should be among the most thought-out aspects of creating a captivating film because if the logline is unclear, then the other elements will be as well. The logline is typically written when you've finished writing your script. The reason for this is that the logline is an edited version of the script that is then distributed to producers, agents and, possibly, other media which can help you win funds to make your film. The logline can help you promote an idea of your film overall and is the reason it is vital to craft an engaging, memorable unique, memorable one. Loglines can be the difference between making or break your career in Hollywood before you begin. It is important to ensure that you don't think of it as an extra-curricular idea.

There are a variety of factors that comprise a successful logline. In the end, it should convey the main narrative, without delving into the intricacies of each person or story. It should not exceed one sentence at minimum; while communicating its readers with the idea of:

1. The principal protagonist. What is the story's focus?
2. The end goal. What is the character trying to achieve?
3. The adversary. Who stands behind the principal character?

The main character

When writing the logline and mention the main character make sure you don't mention the character's name as it could make the reader confused while reading your logline. One exception is when your story concerns the most important historical figure or public persona. Instead of the name of the character, refer to a relatable job or the status of the protagonist, for example, a an entrepreneur and American president. One of the biggest errors that screenwriters who are amateurs make is to use their characters as their own voices of reasoning. Even if you're creating a story that is influenced by your own personal experiences or struggles, it's essential to make your the main character their own identity. They shouldn't be doing or feeling things because of the way you feel, or the way you react to a particular circumstance. Keep in mind that even famous persons' biography have to be changed to give them an dramatic edge. When writing personal narratives, certain aspects need to be enhanced even slightly bit to ensure your story can be effective.

If you're working with your primary character, you may also include a carefully selected adjective to the main character which plays a crucial role for defining who the character is the people who will be watching. Examples:

"Brave soldier"

"Career---minded executive"

The Objective

The heart of the screenplay is the primary protagonist's goals, which should be clearly stated through the story's logline. The whole tension of the story revolves to the goals and the challenges faced by the protagonist as they strive to accomplish it. The primary goal should be revealed in the first stage of the screenplay whether it's a mental and physical objective.

The Opposition

The antagonists are the elements of the story that hinder the protagonist from achieving his goals. When writing about your opponent make sure not to provide too many details regarding the opponent, but give readers the idea that death or loss is the most likely outcome.

While you're there, is it important to be aware of the most frequent mistakes that writers make when they write their logline. Beware of these mistakes at all costs!

* Too complex. Even in a film that is as complex and has numerous layers like Inception the writer must be able to convey the essence. The logline should be able to concisely and effectively convey the complete idea that the whole basis of your story rests.

* No external quest. People want to witness the transition from the internal

quest to the outside. However, remember that all inner quests share the same premise the same: heroes all want to attain some kind of satisfaction or accomplishment. You've probably noticed that virtually every movie is based on a story where the protagonist transforms from child to adult, an age-related kind of idea. This is what the audience wants to know about, how they achieved it and what they did to succeed.

Lack of conflict. Many filmmakers don't realize the fact that conflict is essential to make the entire film appealing at all. We've all had our own experience that living life is hard and difficult But why would you pay your money to watch an actor rise to fame and be successful in a way that isn't the things you do in your daily routine? We must understand that the hero has be required to undertake a task that is challenging enough to accomplish their objective. Think about whether your quest seem too difficult? Do you think the objective is unattainable to attain? Do you find the conflict to be daunting? If the answers to these questions is non, then you can boost the intensity of conflict by increasing the strength of your opponent or decreasing the strength of the principal persona.

* Isn't original enough. People want to see something new that they've never experienced before. Try to create new ideas; things that aren't expected even with characters that are cliche. You must be familiar with a wide range of movies so that you can tell from this point on if your story is a re-telling of something already made. Better to get external validation. Present your story to colleagues and acquaintances and ask whether they think it's reminiscent of something familiar. If the answer is yes, adjust the elements of your narrative to make it stand out.

It can be difficult for novice scriptwriters to craft an engaging logline that can assist you in selling your script to agents and producers. Making a concise and succinct logline that is exciting isn't simple. However, it requires lots of practice, so put in the time to create an efficient logline. One of the best tips I can offer to you when writing a logline is to get exposed to the most loglines you can. Explore books, films and classic films and even reviews of movies.

Knowing the creative process of writers who created meaningful loglines can assist you to write your own and, eventually, you'll have it down. At the beginning of creating your logline, you might realize that it's written as more than a single sentence and becomes difficult to comprehend. I recommend that you let it be as is for a couple of days and then think about it. Return to it and remove all words you believe don't contribute to the overall tone or the heart to the tale. It will eventually be cut down to its basic base, and you will end up with a phrase that summarizes the plot's
essence.

Chapter 3: The 3 Act Structure

The three-act framework is what which binds your screenplay. The three elements are separated into three parts: confrontation, setup and resolution. These are the main elements of your story. The best stories are based on this three-act structure. it is the foundation for creating an efficient script. Your story as well as your scenes must adhere to it.

The three-act structure is a well-known model that can be seen in novels, plays films, poetry as well as video games. The first time it was thought of was by Aristotle in his Poetics. This kind of structure can be seen throughout the writings of the historical giants like Shakespeare, Hitchcock, and Aristotle. It's a tried and true method that is a proven and reliable to create your film and putting it all together. It's a highly effective method, and I wouldn't suggest straying from this format that can result in a huge disappointment for the potential producers and also your viewers.

Act 1. Setup

The set-up is the first half of the story. It is the time when the principal characters introduce themselves to viewers. It is known as the exposition. It is used to communicate viewers what the entire narrative is. The set-up also provides the dramatic scene and the story's context. This section of your story will answer the questions of who and what, what time, and where, but does not reveal the reasons. Also, it should clearly convey to the reader what the main issues of the main character and also establish their goals. Let your audience feel connected to the character. You'll know you've accomplished an excellent job in creating Act 1, when the audience develops a sense of empathy for the character.

The scene also has an incident that triggers the story, which is an event that sets the story's plot in motion. The most common rule of thumb to keep the attention of your viewers is to introduce the main character as well as the other characters within the initial 10 minutes of the film. If you force them to take longer to wait they may become bored or lose interest in them.

Act 2 - Conflict

The final confrontation is the longest section of your script. It takes about 60 minutes. If Act 1 exposes your character's motivations then Act 2 will include your character in pursuit of their aim. In Act 2 the main characters will also encounter their romantic partners who they may have and the mentors who will support them for the remainder in the story. It is also the time when the protagonist will have to confront those obstacles or the environments that can pose a challenge for him. As the conflict develops and escalates, more risk or danger present to the protagonist. In essence, the tension between the main character and his adversary will be evidently felt.

The battle also includes the initial culmination point, in which the main character appears as if they're close to achieving their goal . However, in mid-point they realize they must do more or else everything else will fall into disarray.

The middle of the story is the one that reveals a moment in the life of the protagonist when they feel they're at their worst and thus, at the most distant achievable stage of achieving their goals. The scene can cause viewers to believe that the primary character will give up eventually. The difficulties your protagonist will have to face in Act 2 helps bring your story to life and in turn, viewers will be more interested in the overall story.

Many writers realize they have to write Act 2 is the most difficult to write and that's where they commit the error of abandoning. Do not! If you're just beginning be aware that it is normal to get stuck for a time and it's going to allow you to think about the story further. One trick that some of the best thinkers in Hollywood have learned when they are stuck is to get into the head of the adversary. In all the time, you might have spent too much time in the protagonist's mind, and this is your chance to change sides for some time bit. A character who has a completely different perspective to your protagonist will provide you with an opportunity to breathe fresh air and give you the new perspective you require to carry on with your story.

Act 3 - Resolution

The resolution is the point at which the story ends by reviving the struggle of the main character's. As you finish your story, be aware that you want your ending to be exciting and yet unpredictably and also fulfill your commitment to the audience. In ideal circumstances, the protagonist is able to achieve something that is pleasing to him, even if it's not always the outcome the character had hoped for, however, the viewer will see it as a satisfactory ending for the narrative.

The resolution is a culmination in which the fight is the highest intensity physically as well as emotionally, causing the audience into their seats in anticipation. The protagonist is going to fail, but you could ingenuously make them fail and attempt again until they succeed however, you make the audience think that the ultimate success of the character isn't possible.

The next stage after the climax is final scene, where peace is restored to the normal state at the beginning. At this point the characters are already transformed as a result of the events and difficulties they've encountered and are now having difficulty in adjusting to the equilibrium.

Since there isn't a definitive way to determine the best way to end scripts the process has become something that is very personal to the writers of Hollywood. The scripts may even end with some twists and the last pages create more dramatic tension. To ensure a successful end, ensure that you have answered these questions:

1. Was the incident that started the conflict resolved or was the initial conflict was it resolved?

2. Was there a second character conflict that was solved?

3. How did you alter your main protagonist from beginning to the final scene in the movie?

The value of the three-act design is because it assists writers create an impressive flow of motion. This, in turn, ensures that everything is happening consistently. Change and movement are important in a well-written screenplay or novel, book or film. You then work from this fundamental concept: hero + obstacles is conflict.

What causes the movement? Conflict, one following the next. Be sure to remain focused on your protagonist or your primary hero, and make sure that he is constantly exploring the new or dangerous terrain in order to expose him to obstacles that are appropriate. Writing a story that is not based on the three-act structure you could think of it as like building a home without the foundation. The walls will begin to sink, your roof to fall and the whole structure will begin to self-destruct.

The final thing you want your viewers to say about your film is that it's boring and

predictable. boring. This is the most common complaint about every bad film. The three-act structure prevents boredom from forming as it allows the writer to identify events and things which cause conflict and changes that creates new conflicts and on until the
Resolution is reached.

Chapter 4: The Main Character

The protagonist of your story must remember, love and respected by your viewers. The protagonist is responsible for telling the story, and guides your readers by the exact same feelings the character experiences.

Character development is vital for every story. They aren't stereotypical, and they should be more complex as the story progresses and when the characters interact. They should be open to emotional change and transformation, and be able to communicate their ideals, values and values through the entire story. The creation of a great main character requires lots of thought and research, since your objective is to create a totally new character. Take into consideration their background as well as their background, biographical as well as their personality, psychology, and goals for their life. The audience should be able to grasp the character's anxieties and motivations and goals. Make use of all your senses to bring life to the main character, as well as any other character in your story. Consider their family background, work physical attributes, as well as their distinct characteristics. It is essential that you are capable of recognizing the person as if you are the person and also that you feel comfortable the inside scoop. You must be able to think about them and understand their personality inside out.

Effective character development is among the most fascinating, yet difficult aspects of writing scripts. It's not easy to not be a bit emotional about the process, as you have to develop a character who can feel something, and not just a one-dimensional puppet with cliché traits. They're not puppets and they're the protagonist of the story. They have to be able to be to life.

The process of writing screenplays demands you, the writer to answer the following question: Why? What role will the character have to take on within the narrative? What do you feel towards the character? Why is your character pursuing what he desires? What is the motivation for your character? It's also crucial to identify the vulnerability of your character's character What are their weaknesses? What's their kryptonite, the thing that can cause their demise? Once you've put the pieces it will be possible to get an interesting story to tell. You'll be able to understand the different paths your character will follow to reach their goals and not fall into weaknesses or what they have to do to prevent their own fall. If you place your character in their situation you're creating the tension-building core to your tale.

The development of a character as the story unfolds is referred by the term "character arc. It's important because when we witness the character's transformation and grow, we experience it through them, and in the end we undergo transformation with the character. Do you not notice that whenever you are watching a good film you are enticed to the protagonist at some point, being a fan until the film ends with the protagonist winning? This is because great films have characters so well-written, that the viewers cannot resist becoming invested in the characters.

Take for instance the film Miss Congeniality. FBI Agent Gracie Hart, played by Sandra Bullock, had the purpose of locating an armed terrorist that was targeting her Miss United States event. To accomplish her objective she needed to covertly become an contestant however Gracie is as a sexy as it gets as well as the FBI team needed to help her discover her feminine side once more. For the majority of her life, she's always part of the boys, however, she was now required to appear more feminine as well as soft and weak, which for her does not make her a great FBI agent. It took some effort her to be the character that of the Madame. United States, and at near the conclusion of the film she was embracing her feminine aspect. Gracie let it empower her and could achieve her goal while changing from beginning to end of the film.

It is important to note that even though your character can be a success in most circumstances but it's equally essential to show him flaws. If he's pure and tidy and doesn't have any bad qualities in any way, he can become dull, uninteresting and insignificant to the viewers. I'll repeat this over and over and repeatedly throughout the book: readers are looking for something they can connect to. And since everyone has imperfections, you would not want one who didn't have it isn't it? Your audience should be able to identify with himand see him succeed and reach the goals he has set for himself as a person. Your audience must have a worry that he might not succeed. If he's the perfect person, there is no doubt.

If there's one thing that the viewers also love is a strong main character. Sometimes, it's not even what they're trying achieve that we love their character, but the lengths to which they'll go to achieve it. He is brave under extreme pressure and in dire circumstances which we would love to do.

Do you remember the film, The Pursuit of Happiness, with Will Smith? While everything seemed to be going well at the beginning of the film however, the protagonist eventually suffers a loss and must come up with inventive ways to enhance his quality of his life as well as himself. He makes steps forward to achieve success, and then he succeeds when he is millionaire.

Change shouldn't occur suddenly. It should be clear right from the start that your character could change, as otherwise it could appear as if it was forced and unlikely. It is helpful to work with the character's arc. can be helpful if you begin at the beginning, then the middle and then the ending, so that you can ensure an evolution that is gradual.

In accordance with the kind of story you're writing Your opponent may be a character in a arc as well. Keep in mind that the character's story doesn't have to be positive, because the drama of the film is often a success with a central character who has a shift to the negative.

Some suggestions for keeping in mind while creating your memorable main character:

1. Give your loved ones an innate sense of humor. Movies are a popular choice for various reasons. Apart of entertainment, we'd like to escape reality , even for a couple of hours. The best method to get away from reality is through laughter So create a character that is fun.

2. Make a character with talent; make him a person with skills that nobody else has.

3. Instill a sense of passion in them that drives them through the whole film.

4. Not the last; we shouldn't put any more importance to what is important to him and his determination to make a change.

Once you've created an important character, they're likely to require someone whose main objective is to stop your main protagonist from achieving in the first place: the antagonist.

Chapter 5: The Opposition

Fantastic stories feature heroes, but they also feature villains. From comics to stories from the past the villain has always played a major part in giving your story an edge. They're the ones responsible for mixing conflict into the storyand serving as a challenge to the protagonist every time. throughout.

A good antagonist is as important for a successful story like the main character. Therefore, you must put enough thought and consideration into your opponent as you do your hero. The presence of a character with opposite motives as your main character can give the story a edge and balanced. If you have thought to your main character, but not the antagonist the script may lack equilibrium, which causes the story to become unbalanced and losing its impact.

Your story may have at least one or two antagonists It is important to create their roles with care to create the tension you desire. A strong opponent will keep the audience on the edge of their seat and eager to learn more about the way in which the story unfolds. The people watching will be hoping that the main character will be able to defeat him. A good story, in the ideal case, will gift the opponent only a few good points. Sometimes, the adversaries start as a side to the protagonist and, in certain circumstances, turn into the character's enemy.

Consider the strengths that the opponent must possess. He must possess specific traits which give him the power over the hero, however, the opponent should also have his own weaknesses. He should also be able to shield himself from the strengths of the main character. To ensure the balance of the story make sure that both the hero as well as the adversary the identical quantity of weaknesses and strengths. The real issue is in the event that you can make the other capitalize on the weaknesses of the other, and the hero becoming triumphant in the final.

At the core the antagonist creates a sense of resentment in the viewers. There are, however, villains who are so adept in their craft that they become memorable and, since the public hates the character so much, he gets a mighty reputation. This is the reason many of us have favourite villains. Some suggestions to think about when you are creating your own opponent:

* The enemy doesn't have to always need necessarily be villainous or even human.

* He must be at a minimum as intelligent or even more effective than his main counterpart

* Each character has their own development, or personal change. In reality, the adversary may be contemplating making a change when the main character gains influence over him, or is more determined. In either case, the struggle could also transform his character towards the final chapter.

* Must be fear-inspiring enough of the protagonist to be feared so that the audience stays at their seat in anticipation of the main character's failings

Always throws challenges the main character's direction and keeps him on his toes, and thinking of strategies to beat the adversary. The opponents can be divided into different types:

Immoral Opponent

This is among the most well-known types of adversaries you can pick from. The difference between them and the hero is as apparent as night and day or both in black and white. This allows viewers to decide which side to support. It could take form of form or a person who is a hypocrite who exudes sweetness, goodness and compassion on the surface , but is actually filled with negative motives. Since the hypocrite is capable of fooling the innocent and the public, they hate the person even more.

The immoral adversary can be portrayed as the psycho, which is composed of pure evil that is unadulterated. Psychos appear in psychological thrillers and psychological dramas as well as in horror stories. They're serial killers, mass-murderers... You can get the picture. They strike fear into the hearts of their viewers as they are scared of them, regardless of whether they're fictional or not. persona.

The morally impure opponent could appear as a normal individual who was a victim of their weaknesses or desire, greed, or an extreme hatred. These feelings could lead them to the situation that puts the life of the main character in danger, which could lead to your battle.

Moral Opponent

The moral adversary is an incredibly complex character due to the fact that he has more layers for readers to unravel and comprehend. They tend to decide to do the right choice, but the conflict in your story demands that they engage in the fight with your protagonist.

He could be a decent person on a team that is different but even though he would do no harm to your heroes, they're standing on two different motives that fuel the fire of conflict and trigger negative emotions. For instance, lawyers who advocate for various causes or the love triangle in which two people fight with the same lady. These kinds of stories could lead to a variety of results pertaining to morality and life's biggest questions.

The moral adversary can be in it's form that of an amoral crusader who can be quite frightening. He is driven by the passion for his cause and when confronted with a choice, he will go in the direction he believes to be the best option. There is also the possibility of an individual who is obsessed by his love of something, which could result in him making dangerous choices, which could put the main persona at risk.

Additionally, he might take on form of form as a regular person, who in desperate need, resorts to illegal ways because they feel there is no other option.

The morally immoral opponent says the fact that all adversaries don't need to be bad. There are many different kinds of opponents and that's why you'll find that in some films, the antagonists aren't necessarily bad. The opponents can further be classified into two groups:

* The Scene Opponent

The main role of the scene's antagonist is to create obstacles to prevent characters from reaching their objective in every scene. The entire thing that the antagonist desires, is completely opposite of what the main character wants. If the antagonist from the scene is present, he creates tension, creating jeopardy and making the audience feel tense. If you plan to use the scene adversary, make sure that, when looking over each scene there is a clear understanding of what the purpose is. Be cautious not to go overboard, because you could make one bad thing occur after another and create an unsatisfactory action film.

*The Big Troublemaker

Big troublemakers are able to alter the course of events and make the main character run for his money. The effect he has on the main character's life is so significant that the audience think that the main character has against the odds of the biggest troublemaker. Although this character does not necessarily need to be frightening but he has a potential that none of the characters in the film does. This creates a great tension, and that's what audiences love about.

It is important to note this, that the main troublemaker doesn't need to be a human. It is a perfect illustration of the weaknesses of the protagonist and could be an issue that is difficult to overcome. It could be an addiction alcohol, as in the movie 28 Days. It can also be a mighty natural disaster, like storms. It could Even in some form of an idea.

Chapter 6: The Supporting Cast

You now know what is that you need to do to create a great screenplay, but the ultimate aim is to write an outstanding screenplay. One that allows people to relate to and discuss the details of the relationships the characters in the film had. This is the place

The role of supporting characters is crucial and they must be as intricate as the main protagonist, but it's also your responsibility to make sure that the main character's character as well as his interaction with the supporting characters are crucial to the story that you are telling. Writers, especially those who are just beginning their careers are prone to overlook the importance of supporting characters as a given. Screenwriting seminars tend to emphasize on the significance of the primary character. But let's face the facts our relationships make us human and surely make our lives more fascinating and interesting, not to mention the fact that they provide multiple dimensions and variations in our daily lives. Particularly our closest friends and our confidants. What would life be like without your friends? Are you able to tell the tale of your life without the support of your friends? Similar to that, do not tell your protagonist's story without their closest friend. The presence of the character's "close friend" will improve the viewers perception on the character and will help them connect with the character on a higher level.

Consider the following close family members, that have had an impact to the people around them:

1. My Very Best Friend's Wedding. What do Julianne have done in the absence of her homosexual best-friend George who she would talk to and confide in with whenever she felt sad? George was a crucial part of her life in lifting her spirits, and made Julianne's character feel happy and even laugh during moments when she believed she was not achieving her character's goals, that was, to marry Michael, her closest friend. Michael.

2. Lethal Weapon. What could Roger have done without his hilarious companion, Roger? The well-known duo have been praised for their ability to entertain audiences so often that it's hard for one to think of one of them.

3. Pretty pretty in Pink. Duckie is one of Andie's closest acquaintances, who appears to be a clown in the movie to hide his feelings for Andie. It's hard not to feel sorry for his character. He ceases talking to Andie after he discovers she's going to marry Blaine.

4. Romy as well as Michelle's reunion at High School. Romy and Michelle are among the most popular film friends duos. They bonded with each other and even debated at times, but at the end, they were an extremely entertaining pair who worked together to achieve the goals of their characters.

One of the best ways to create a strong character supporting the main character by using a close friends is to create conflict between their personality. The function of a close person to the principal character is to offer emotional support and believe to the protagonist. They giving them the tools needed to be successful, encourage them, and possibly enhance their own stake to the narrative. In the course of the main character's struggle as well as when they're down or when they encounter struggles, audiences are eager watching how their best companion or friend pushes them to keep going, since that's exactly what they're made to do.

Here are some examples of the most well-known supporting characters you may like to incorporate in your story:

1. The person who is the party. She is able to play the character's primary interests, especially when the main character is an introverted, shy role. Sometimes, she'll even say things the character could say, assisting in putting crucial elements of the film. The party girl may take the form of someone who will even encourage the protagonist to get into trouble. Do you remember that show called Wedding Crashers? Jeremy and John play best friends who host parties with each other,

and are in lots of trouble. In the film Black Swan, the role was played well by Mila Kunis. She helped Natalie Portman's character to confront her dark, fearful fears.

2. Mother figure. The mother figure, also known as a mentor is the one who plays the role as a wise and charming guide to the protagonist. She offers practical suggestions on how the protagonist should accomplish her goals, and occasionally even dies in the hope of moving this story forward. An excellent example is Aunt May of The Amazing Spiderman.

3. The doormat. This is one kind of character that is often the main brain behind the story's underlying operations. They are the ones who create plans and also do the expository work to the protagonist and can also have characters who are passive that causes the main character to overlook them at times. A doormat can be described as a logical close companion who attempts to make things happen to develop the character and grow. Ron Weasley in the Harry Potter

series is an excellent illustration of the doormat.

4. Father figure. If your character is flawed due to the fact that they had a father figure who died in their youth or ignored him, or abandoned him behind, the father figure is an important role in supporting the character because the father figure fills in that gap. Through his support the main character will be able to achieve his goals. One example of the supportive role of the father figure would be the character of Alfred in the Batman films.

Because your protagonist has their own weaknesses and weaknesses, having a most trusted friend is an important element that adds the character and depth for your tale. They take on the form of people who we would meet in the real world even if it's only the bartender who your protagonist visits each when he feels they are hindering him from achieving his goals. Find inspiration but also seek out a purpose when you create the most trustworthy friend or trusted character.

Making a character is hard enough, especially if you're starting out. Now imagine you're required to come up with a lot of characters. The trick is to stop your secondary characters from looking like cookie cutters. They must be as engaging as your principal characters. Check out these suggestions to create memorable characters for your secondary characters:

* Create the illusion of an arch. In contrast to the main characters who's character arcs must be planned much more meticulously and crafted, supporting characters could change in throughout the film without explanation. At the end of 100 pages, your character could be hateful of children, and a couple hundred pages later, all suddenly he is a fan of children. This is perfectly fine.

Introduce your characters in two crucial sequences from the film. The first one should be set in the background, and the second one should be in the front. The first time that your audience gets to meet the protagonist's closest friend, it may be in passing, however later on , you'll be able to give more information that will provide more details about why their contribution is vital in helping the main character reach their objective. In the second part of the introduction, the audience might not immediately recognize the character, but they'll be able to experience that moment of illumination which helps them identify the character, and will later assist them in putting this story. This creates a feeling of familiarity. The audience may have only seen an individual before , but it is now closer to understanding the story in the narrative.

* Connect them to an area, so that every time the viewer comes upon that specific place, they are already familiar with the companion or character. The location could be anyplace like a favourite café or beach or even a bar. A place that is their own makes their character appear more authentic.

• Work on creating flaws in the character of your choice just as you would the main character and adversary. Nothing is more unremarkable in a film than a character with none flaws, or tries to be perfect and perfect. It becomes boring very quickly. Similar to that having a character who has flaws doesn't make it appear as if you're trying to convince them to become the mouthpiece of the writer and be part of dialog of the film. Make sure that you do something that the viewers will remember, for example, offering them a distinctive way of speaking or the ability to identify flaws, such as damaging or bad behavior.

Your character must be able to demonstrate at least one distinctive characteristic. Like the best friends in our real lives, every person around us has a distinct trait that

We are awed by them and love them.

Chapter 7: Love Interest

The love interest does not have to be real however it's what the protagonist is willing to fight for or portrays as the most important passion in the film. It is the love of the primary character's aim, what they want to accomplish by when they finish the film and that is as obvious as night and day.

The biggest errors writers make when they begin is to give the protagonist a very vague purpose. I've actually read screenplays where the protagonist is just a flittering from one place to the next and then, in a flash is over with the story. They did nothing that was significant. If such stories were to be shown on large screens, the viewers will not have any idea exactly what it really about, since the main character didn't actually make any changes to the course of his life. Yes, your audience is likely to be distracted by boredom.

Imagine your situation this way: If someone asks you to define what the goal of the protagonist is, refrain from giving vague responses like "to be with one of the girls in his desires" or "to be happy" or "to attain the goal of financial freedom". Because these responses are unclear, it is difficult to tell if he could actually achieve the goals. What you need is an objective that is tangible for the principal character, since you want readers to be able to support him to see it come to completion no matter what it is to achieve it. What is it that you want the character you've created to feel satisfied? What are the requirements to be happy to be in an intimate relationship with the woman of his desires? What should he accomplish to become wealthy and successful? These are the questions you should think about.

The love of the protagonist, or the primary desire of the character, is what is the main focus of the story. Although characters might have distinct needs in different scenes but they all have one main goal, which differs from what they would like. Sometimes characters are unaware of the requirement. This is why it's crucial to define what they want and what they require. Let's break this down even more.

When you are working towards your way to the main character's objective it is a desire that they are aware of. This desire usually comes out during the opening act in which the protagonist can express their desire to "want to win the game" or "want to impress that girl" or "catch the villain". But, the primary character's motivation can change as an additional goal emerges. This isn't a new goal it's merely a necessity that surfaces.

The desire is external, while the desire is inside. Be aware of that. In simple terms the need of the protagonist is what is the basis of the character's whole that is what he's comprised of, or a portion of it that's been suppressed for a long time. It is in conjunction with the character's desire in defining their purpose. This is evident in numerous films, where on the surface, the character appears to be a solitary and whose personality changes when an event draws them closer to their inner self that reveals their love for or more human.

Likely, the adversaries has their own objectives at the start. Maybe one desires to work without interruption or have a good night's sleep. It could be as easy as that. But the events that occur throughout the film could turn their lives upside down, causing them to fight head-on when they try to satisfy their own goals and desires. The lives of both the protagonist and antagonist are then removed from their respective lives to embark on a journey they never imagined they'd be on begin with.

Examples of the difference between needs and wants:

Man grieves over the death by his dad, but he realizes that he needs to get justice in return by looking for the guilty murderer to prevent him from harming his brother.

* A woman is looking for her father's identity However, she is forced to go home after more than 25 years there.

A former police officer seeks to locate an alleged serial killer that's planning to set off a bomb, however, he's only got five days to complete the task and must be a fervent investigator.

While writing your script, you'll continually be asked what your character's goal. Their actions will be guided on their motivation and their love interest and their goals, with their personality characteristics that you've identified.

They were assigned to them after you created the character you chose to draw.

Chapter 8: Accelerating Moment

The "Something big Happens" is also known as the hook, is the defining point of your screenplay. It's the one you'll be using to present your screenplay, and show to producers that your script is profitable.

The ideal hook should be set within the initial five paragraphs of the screenplay. Since the MTV generation, viewers have seen their attention spans shrink and for the screenwriter, this means that you need to keep the audience interested within a shorter amount of time. This means that you must make sure that the story is moving. The genres of suspense, horror and crime fiction have all used murder or death as a representation of what happens when something major happens however, because this has been done numerous times, it's now a cliche. If you choose to make use of this technique, be sure the remainder of the story is an engaging one. Some other popular kinds of major events include the impact of a meteor on earth and similar to that. You get it.

Learn how to write hooks, but also how to create a strong one. A strong hook can cause the reader to inquire. Be sure the question is pertinent and is related to the remainder of your story.

Let's take a look at a well-known example: The movie Silence of the Lambs in which the brand young FBI woman, Clarice, is tossed into the world of psychopaths. This is a great hook since it makes you wonder whether Clarice is able to successfully find information while remaining alive. In the 1995 film Swingers which is about an ensemble of friends living in Hollywood and are faced with dating issues There is a subdued attraction in form of asking the audience ask if Mike might end up breaking down and calling that girl who he's oozing with. The question is a part of the rest of the story as the character of Mike develops which allows it to be seamlessly integrated with the the script. It's possible to be as bold as want; think about Betty Blue: the movie begins with the protagonists naked, walking into their beach home and getting in the midst of passionate moments of romance. That's the kind of story that draws the attention of viewers for your tale. Rewind to all your most loved films in every genre, and ask yourself: at which point did the film truly grab your attention? Review the way the films began. As the screenwriter, you are able to produce the same effect with the very first screenplay you write. Writing, you'll be able to define the mood, make the appropriate tones and draw your viewers into the story through the setting of an important event that they will not be able to shake out of their minds until the movie is able to help to answer an issue. It's a crucial sequence of events and scenes that guide readers through the rest of your story. It provides a motive for the final scene and end. When they experience this hook scene, your viewer realizes that by the time the film is over the problem is resolved by the antagonist, the protagonist or even the main and central issue.

Writers who aren't professionals tend to fall into the trap of wasting their first pages by filling them with boring dialogue. Don't make the same error. The first few pages are as important, if perhaps more, since that's the reason viewers will stick around to enjoy your film instead of leaving in boredom.

Chapter 9: Emotional Decision

The protagonist has to react to the incident, and this means that they must take action that they don't feel enthusiastic about. This call to action,, also known as the incident that triggered it is essentially an event that dramatically alters the character's life.

For instance, the movie Armageddon that has several thrilling scenes. In the beginning you could think the moment to act was when the first meteor destroyed the Space Shuttle, eventually striking the earth. It could also be the time where Truman was able to discover the grave negative consequences of the asteroid size of Texas that is en route to the earth. Nothing of the above! The actual call to action in this case is when Harry Stamper, played by Bruce Willis, was summoned to be a part of NASA. This was a decision that he was required to take to satisfy his needs even though he and his family members were scared.

A call for action may be termed"the calling to adventure specifically because, as I've mentioned, it's an event that pushes the protagonist out of his comfortable zone. It can help the audience understand the primary goal of the character. A call-to-action does not necessarily need to be a massive and significant incident. It could be as straightforward as a phone call however, this section of the script plays an crucial role in the remainder of the movie. It is the catalyst that sets the wheels turning through the minds of the viewers of what the final scene could look in.

It's impossible to tell an engaging story without the need to take action. Should you have done that, will end up being is a bunch of characters scurrying around without a purpose in sight. You may be thinking what exactly happens when this call for action take place?

In some genres and stories in certain genres, the call to action might be made before the film begins, though that's uncommon. In the majority of cases it occurs in the initial 28 pages in your story however to the audience it happens after you've introduced the protagonist, and showed to the viewers how his story is like. It can also happen following the introduction. In the film Rocky The inciting event was extremely late. The main character is likely to respond to the prompt and might even be able to resist till Act One breaks. This is followed by luring the audience and then the hero is able to commit to the journey. The story could be physical, mental, emotional or even a mix of all three.

It is important to remember when creating your character's call-to-action: it is not an active moment, but something that occurs in your characters. It's not something the character actively pursues or participates in. The first part of the story would typically involve the protagonist dealing to the consequences of an incident, however, at some point, he will have to decide if he's going to go deeper or not.

The incident that triggers the film from a calm structure to one that is chaotic. Consider it the point at which there is no turning back. Following the incident that triggered it There is no way to be restored to normality unless the protagonist achieves his purpose. It's now time to ask yourself What exactly do your characters would like? What's holding them back from achieving it?

If your character is successful in his quest, it's an enjoyable conclusion. However, if he fails the story is a tragedy or an action. The event that triggers the incident will cause your audience to reflect on the question. This triggers actions in place, and it triggers the speculation of whether the team they're rooting for is going to win or not.

Examples of incidents that are incitement-inducing:

Legally Blonde. In the year Warner ended his relationship with Elle and she was waiting for him to propos to her.

* Gladiator. The time Marcus Aurelius, the emperor asked for Maximus to serve as Rome's Steward.

The Chronicles of Narnia. Lucy's discovery that her wardrobe is the key to her success will lead her back to Narnia.

*Clockwork Orange. When Georgie suggests that the group be able to pull off a real heist in response to Alex

* Star Wars. When Luke Skywalker spots the digital picture of the Princess Leia in need of help, he asks her for assistance

* Alien. If the crew is able to land upon the surface of the earth, but discovers an abandoned, destroyed spacecraft from another planet

* Jerry Maguire. When Jerry places his Mission Statement on the mailbox of all the employees but he is not sure of his thoughts . What is a great trigger? It can cause the audience to flashback to the events that preceded it in the film and come to realize that everything they believed would occur or was true was actually not the case. The key to this is keeping the viewer on edge, and to be wary of predictability at all costs.

Some suggestions for hints to keep in mind when writing about the incident that triggered it:

1. Don't keep the audience waiting for too long.

Rocky was a cult film that featured a late inciting incident that was a success because it was written by experienced scriptwriters. It is important to take slow steps to understand how to properly pace your characters as well as the events in the film. Use the fundamental formula of writing inciting scenes earlier in the film, since this is what keeps your audience interested in the film.

2. This is the storyline which will be the driving force part of the tale, thus ensure it's engaging and captivating.

The audience should be aware of what will happen following the character's response or declines to take act. Does the detective be treated the same way like the others? Are they going to catch the culprit? The audience should be riveted on their chairs.

3. Not the last, ensure that it's credible.

Don't make decisions that make your audience think: " Why on earth did they do this? ?" If the call to action isn't convincing it will be a loss for your audience interest right away.
away.

Chapter 10: The Main Character's Goal

This is the perfect time to think about the purpose of your character. You must consider the kind of change you wish to be able to see in your character. What sort of improvements over their current state do you wish to see? What kind of improvements are they required to reach their goals? What do they must do in order to get back to a time that was better than they are?

The objective is crucial for the protagonist which is why they try to hold onto it with a lot of vigor despite numerous challenges and emotional setbacks they will encounter during the film.

The main characters in well-crafted stories might even have two major objectives. The first is the story objective which is shared by all others in the film. This goal impacts all the characters. Also, there is the personal conflict, or the personal goals. The reason why is that they're the primary characters is due to the fact that they make decisions which help them to solve their personal conflicts. This option also has a role to be played in determining the way in which the story's overall is resolved.

A few examples from the most famous films:

*In Star Wars, when Luke Skywalker decides to follow his instincts instead of his computer, it aids him in defeating The Death Star.

* If Romeo and Juliet decide to take their own lives rather than to live a life without their partner This leads to an agreement between their families.

There are other stories in which the main character may not have an inner conflict, however you'll find that these films tend to be lacking in emotional depth. However stories without an objective can paint the picture of a character who's emotionally charged but fails to provide any form to the purpose of the film. The result is a film which is a bit unfocused, and then, in the end, useless.

If you're writing an extended film, it is possible to assign your main character extra objectives, which are often referred to as subplots. However, when you write these subplots, ensure you think about them carefully in order to make sure they are significant impact on the main plot.

As we're discussing the subject also, I'd like to mention that not only must the main character or main character have a mission however, the adversary should also have a goal. The objectives of the opponent should not be at odds with the goals of the main character.

Here are the reasons the main character's goals are essential to the story you write:

1. Goals can tighten the plot.

There are films or scripts in which you've ended with the question "Where is the story going in that?" A plot that appears to be lost, or without an end in sight, is that doesn't have clear goals for the characters. If your viewers ask this question, it means that the plot is weak and you didn't do your task as a writer. The only reason that an audience can legitimately ask the question is if that was your intention at all to deceive them in order to take them off guard.

It is important to set clear objectives for the main character since this will prevent you from getting scenes that slow the whole plot. A tightly-planned plot can stop your readers from having to take breaks. break as your audience will be too very much about leaving the story in its entirety.

2. A strong character goal makes your story credible.

If you're just beginning it's normal to have a number of scenes that don't actually have any objectives. When you're rewriting your initial drafts it's essential to address these problems. For instance, if your character keeps getting into trouble without being resolved it will grow insane fast, and the readers is likely to become bored. This is due to the fact that there are no goals to guide the story. After a while these issues will keep growing on top of one another and will not be logical.

3. Having character goals can help simplify your workload. This is because when your character's goals are clearly defined this will be their primary motivation and keep

them focused throughout various scenes. The protagonist will be contemplating their goal instead of having a dialogue with other characters over useless problems.

In lieu of needing to constantly consider how to place your character into certain scenes, keeping that objective in mind will lessen your stress and allow you to think about the best way to accomplish this. You character will be working towards their objectives, and taking the steps they have to take in order to achieve what they're aiming to achieve.

While writing it, you should establish the goals of your character in the beginning. In time, you'll realize that you'd like to alter the goals, which is fine. If the goal of your character changes it is also necessary to be willing to alter the story's outcome.

Goals needn't necessarily be difficult. They could be huge and even tiny, but the most important thing is that you have enough of them in order to make sure that there is tension throughout the story. The aim can be joyful or sad, thrilling scary, or terrifying, since the whole story revolves around what happens to the character who achieves the objective.

If you assign your characters a purpose you're providing them with a reason to exist. It's the reason they're in the story to begin with. To reach the goal, there'll have to be obstacles to over, which will create the tangle of tension within the story. There is no formula that outlines any specific guidelines for how characters reach their goals, and it is up to the author. Be patient with yourself Don't give yourself too difficult a time when you are creating obstacles. The viewers will appreciate the fight and so should you.

A final tip to consider when designing the conflict and goal Just make sure your character isn't sailing through life with ease. You need them to be relatable and let's face it, real life can be difficult. Your character will face challenges on their way to success the same way we face when trying to complete a difficult task.

Chapter 11: Genre

In essence the genre is by the elements of the narrative

Based on this, the story's structure is constructed. It is important to know the story you'll be writing as it is the basis for making an

A compelling script and a sellable story requires you to be careful about managing the expectations of your audience.

A majority of genres in film are borrowed from literary genres which categorize films into the following categories:

The action genre is generally marked by intense chases and physical action battle scenes, as well as continuous motion. In short the action genre is in which continuous physical action is the precedence over storytelling or , in other words, they do the job of telling stories. These kinds of films typically features a protagonist who is pursuing a goal of such great importance that it seems impossible to accomplish it.

* Adventure films are thrilling in that they keep the viewers' attention by putting the

characters in exotic locales, or putting them in thrilling situations. In the genre of adventure the main character is placed at the center of a major battle or adventure, in order to find something new to them. The plot usually is infused with suspenseful scenes that are multiple and puzzles to solve.

* Comedies are movies which aim to entertain viewers through humorous plots, and other strategies that involve the use of language, humor, sarcasm and over-the-top situations in characters. There are numerous forms of comedic styles that you can pick from, such as romance comedies as well as slapstick parodies, spoofs, and dark comedies that are satirical. Comedy films can contain serious material but generally speaking, the conclusion is typically an enjoyable one.

* Gangster and crime films are based on how mobsters live their lives and criminals. They can take on the form of criminals or robbers. They are basically those who are able to operate without regard to law to pursue their own style of

living. Films about crime usually focus on an individual's life as a prominent criminal or mobster or tell the tale of his ascendancy and decline, fights with law enforcement, or even rival groups. These kinds of films are typically set in dense cities, to provide an insight into the lives of the criminal who lives in the shadows.

"Drama" films tend to be emotional, serious and thought-provoking movies. The characters are based on real-life problems and tensions with real-life characters generally, people who the audience can easily identify with. In contrast to other genres, they do not make use of action, special effects, or humor to get their idea across. The characters depicted often need to confront a major struggle with the external forces either human or non-human. Dramatic films usually encompass a variety of subjects that touch on human experience. It may be about racial discrimination or societal issues and addiction to drugs and alcoholism, religious intolerance, mental illness, violence or other similar subjects.

* Epics, also known as historical films typically focus on the past or a fictional incident; and the story is based on mythological characters legendary, mythical, or heroic type. The characters are set in exotic locations, wearing extravagant costumes when they are in films of the past, as well as background music also plays an important role in telling the story of a moment during the time of. The sets are huge and intricate and use an abundance of actors to create that historical feel in the old cities and towns.

* Horror films have one objective in mind: to inflict as much terror and terror into the hearts of the viewers. The genres of films that are a part of them expose the underlying fears that we have been avoiding and bring us to our knees in the frightening manner. Horror films are dark, and tell stories through strange and bizarre events that may be non-fiction or fictional. Horror films can be a good fit

with science fiction, especially when they employ aliens or other terrifying monsters that don't exist, and utilize special effects to address supernatural themes like those of the dead witches, vampires, and various others gothic aspects. The modern horror films typically include using Satanic and negative elements, ghosts that are hostile to people or poltergeists, as well as haunted homes.

* Dance and musical films are cinematic films in which characters tell the story through full-on dancing and singing routine. The narrative in the film typically contains musical scenes within the story, or some scenes require the actors to break into song in unplanned moments. Musicals that are traditional consist of specially selected cast members who perform the sign as their way of telling their story. Of all genres, musicals are thought to be the most escapist of genres and have the goal of the characters generally seeking attraction, fame, and acceptance, or even wealth.

* Science fiction films feature the entire ensemble of special effects characters, heroes, villains exotic locales and futuristic technology, undiscovered forces, and an imaginative production design that makes the locations and characters appear real. Science fiction films usually are set in a period or place other than present day and include travel far away planets and time travel and even elements of fantasy.

It is also essential to know about the various kinds of genres since you do not want to confuse readers. If you're new to the field, it's recommended to stick to the genre you're comfortable with and one you're already familiar with because you're familiar with the style of writing that the genres can provide.

The genre you choose will reflect a particular view and outlook on your story that you're looking tell, though it may not necessarily reflect your personal viewpoint. The genres mentioned above can tell the story in various ways. For instance, if seeking to present the tale of a plane about in danger of colliding, you are able to tell it from a variety of perspectives. It could include a humorous, lighthearted approach to telling the story that's enough to fit into the category of comedy. It might even be dramatic, a kind of film that causes people to contemplate life and death issues. As you can see the choice of the film genre is actually focused on the subject you want to convey to your viewers.

The trick is to tell a story that is accessible, no matter the genre you pick. The best stories reveal something about our human condition. In horror films we are forced confront our most feared fears. Drama is where we are able to look at different aspects of ourselves and what situations might affect us. You can now see how.
point, right?

Chapter 12: Theme

Have you heard anyone complaining about watching a film that makes it seem as if they've seen it before, but using different characters or different settings? It's because films typically are based on a set number of themes. However, it's the manner in which it is presented that is different. The biggest challenge is how as the storyteller can interpret a notion that's been presented in various ways and make the world go wild through your own interpretation of it.

The overall theme of your story is crucial to the overall screenplay. The main goal should be to uncover the truth behind it, or moral, or to express the story that the screenwriter is trying to convey. The most effective themes are created by screenwriters who have seen something for themselves, since these kinds of films are driven by a passion that shines through their characters. Find out what is your passion and use it to propel your story.

The main idea, or the reason for the story is the main point you wish your viewers to understand once they've watched the film. It provides the basis for the rest of the story, which is the reason having a thorough understanding of it is vital to the effectiveness of the overall narrative. It is one of the most costly mistakes made by novice writers: not spending enough time in gaining a complete understanding of the subject they wish to tell. Once you've got a better understanding of your subject take a note of it in a post-it. It can be difficult due to the fact that you're trying to reduce it to its essence. Post it where you want to keep you reminded of the main idea and the theme of your screenplay.

When you've mastered the theme of your story, you'll need to tie together all the components of your story to ensure that all of it reflects an identical moral.

Let's take a look at the main themes in movies:

1. Good versus Evil. This is the primary battle which is seen in numerous comics movies, films, as well as in our own

cultural milieu. Good is defined by characters who show respect, loyalty and courage, while the opposite is represented by characters that display selfishness and prone to betrayal and apathetic. Films with this kind of central theme generally demonstrate that good prevails However, there are certain well-written films in which evil prevails for example, like the case in Star Wars Episode V. The theme of good versus evil is a well-known theme in films because it demonstrates the ultimate battle between characters who are stark opposites.

2. Love overpowers all.

Everybody loves a great love story And Hollywood will never be devoid of stories about love. It is a great fit for any genre because we believe that love is the most noble goal of men. It is the most powerful power in the world and is the most powerful and compelling subject you could utilize to tell a story.

3. Triumph over hardship.

Most films have characters that need to overcome the midst of a challenging situation. If they manage to achieve their goal and win, it's not a surprise that people leave the theater happy because they were cheering on the protagonist to prevail. Films that revolve around this theme are often characterized by the difficulty which is the primary character's story like in the film Slumdog Millionaire. It is almost always about someone with noble intentions and a positive outlook who was thrown into difficult circumstances, but who triumphs over the odds. People enjoy these types of films due to the fact that they portray the human spirit that is unbeatable when faced with difficult situations.

4. Man Vs. Society.

If a person is able to break traditional norms or social customs and traditions, it can make great stories, particularly when you have a principal character who gives up his dignity in the name of fighting for the cause. An excellent example is Erin Brockovich, a woman who used every resource she had to take on an energy company that caused people to be poisoned. The characters generally sacrifice what they can in order to achieve their objectives in the film in order to maintain the social norms or to fight social injustices.

5. Death as a part to the cycles of existence. Death is among the most emotional and threatening themes you can choose to use as the focus of your story. It could be the loss of a member of the family or spouse, child, or even pet. And If the tale is told with care, it will surely strike an emotional nerve. In the movie Hachiko which is about the dog of a person who was killed and the dog never stopped in his search for his owner's return at that same station after his passing. It is a story about affection and love for one another that dogs have for their owners. And you'd be hard-pressed to see any tears after watching the film. Films may explore topics which deal with loss and grief and integrate the subject matter into the film's story, while also successfully telling the story.

6. Revenge.

A very loved themes is revenge. the outcome can differ. In some films where the antagonists are justified, like In Mean Girls, or the person who is seeking revenge can make the situation less favorable for the protagonist, as in Carrie. Whatever the outcome is, revenge movies are all about the process of gaining the right to feel whatever it is, regardless of whether you're the one who's being wounded or the one who hurts others.

7. The process of coming of age.

This is a well-known theme which centers on an innocent main character that must face the adult world with its many complexities and difficulties. Sometimes, they're thrown in by chance and they're not ready to take on what happens to them, like in Juno. In other instances, the protagonist may be more than excited to enter the adult world, as In Sixteen Candles. The theme of coming of age can be used to create an easier plot, like the character undergoing social expectations as well as trying to break out of the introversion phase to be accepted by going to parties or drinking with his friends. However it can be a good idea to incorporate more serious issues like how death, trauma divorce, death, or abuse can alter the character of a person and push them to mature.

8. Man against. Nature.

There is always a fascination in the way man is able to overcome the forces of Nature in and of itself, particularly when they threaten to destroy the human race until characters improve or find the best solution. We are awestruck by movies that focus on the apocalyp and also films that depict people facing the forces of nature, like the case of Jaws.

Chapter 13: Examining Your Book's Potential As A Film Or Series

Before you begin pitching your book to agents or producers before you begin creating a treatment script, and create the film based on your book review your book in a critical manner. It should be clear for it to be turned into the form of a series or film, because some books do not lend themselves for filmmaking.

The process of considering is similar to looking at your book's strengths as well as weaknesses book by using what people in the film industry refer to as "coverage." Once I've finished explaining this, I'll provide fundamental factors to take into consideration. In the next section, I'll present examples of book-to-film reviews that I've written to show how you can analyze the book in order to make a decision.

What is coverage?

A script coverage summarises and evaluates the plot or the narrative of the documentary, as in assessing the script quality. It usually includes 3-4 pages of notes that include the following:

*an indication of the script's author, with the author's name, title the genre of materiallike a feature, an episode of the series or documentary, local or time at which the events take place (in in the moment or in the historical timeframe) and the type of material (i.e. : sci-fi, action/adventure, drama).

A logline is a single sentence outline of the tale

*a brief summary of the tale, which includes the general plot along with the major events, as well as principal characters.

A review of the screenplay's various components which include the story's concept story structure, development and structure characters, dialogue, style of writing; it highlights the strengths and the areas that are in need of improvement.

*Most likely it will be a budget-friendly script

Overall analysis and suggestions on how the script might be made into a film or not, and if it should be.

When the analysis is performed by a professional critic The reviewer will evaluate the main categories of the script by evaluating the main elements -- the premise and storyline, characterisation as well as other important elements - - as to good, excellent fair, poor, or excellent. The reviewer will typically provide a suggestion for what to do with the film, like recommending production, think about as an option, or even pass depending on the following factors:

*Recommendation: The author feels the script is robust and should certainly be written.

It is thought by the reader that the script has many positive points that can be developed into a successful film or series, even though there are some issues that must be solved before it can be suitable to be made.

*Pass: The reader believes that the script is not acceptable, because it's weak in a lot of areas, and should not be written.

Principal considerations in the Book to Film Review

Here are some suggestions to consider when deciding whether your book can be made in a film series.

1.) Which main protagonists exist?

A stand-alone film that runs between 80 and 120 minutes, you typically need two or more principal characters so that the viewers can relate to their story and the characters they portray. There might be a subplot with two or more main characters, however, typically they're supporting characters or antagonists whose story highlights the struggles that the main characters have to face.

If there are several characters with a complicated plot, it could make a great film series that has 3 or more seasons lasting 30 to 90 minutes each.

2.) Does the book have a solid plot with dialogue and action?

Does the book contain an abundance of thinking and reflection through the characters, or an abundance of explanations and debate of concepts?

The most straightforward books to transform into films are those where the story is told via dialog and action, as it's the best thing to show on screen. If the story involves lots of feeling, thinking and reflection, it isn't a good fit for the screen since all thoughts or emotions must be expressed through dialog with another person, in narration over a voice, or by a person who is thinking about himself and speaking to himself. many of these could slow the pace of the plot. However when it's possible to eliminate a lot of this in the film then that's great.

It could also be a problem if a book contains a lot of explanation or discussions on the scientific concept, political and social concepts, or about how specific equipment functions. Discussion and explanations of this kind can be acceptable in a book, however the presence of a lot of it does not work in the form of a film. It's okay to give the viewer with a brief explanation, or a statements of principles or show some brand new technology with a short explanation. However, a long description of the equipment can slow down a film. Also in a book there are instances where characters present the same concept or point of view or even a new technique repeatedly to different characters in various situations This is good for emphasis or real-world realism in the form of a book. However, in a film the repetition of information can be detrimental to the plot and is dealt with by cutting as the character begins to explain or demonstrate something.

So, when you are thinking about making your book film, consider how it can be reduced and cut down so the film will focus on the action and dialogue, even though it could also incorporate reflection and presentations of concepts perspectives, as well as different processes and procedures.

3) What are the locations included in the movie? In what distance are they?

The amount of locations used is a major factor in determining the price of the film. Each location requires a different setting up and taking down of equipment. This could be a couple of hours for an independent filmcertainly much more so when making a feature film that has numerous film cameras and recording gear along with various other materials to be transported. If there are multiple rooms in a house each requires an entirely different setup except when it's being shot with a hand-held camera or on a moving dolly.

If the locations are another house, outside location, or town, it is necessary to include travel time between the locations, and also plan for a different setup. If both locations are close enough, the actors and crew will be able to drive. If the locations are far enough, they should add the travel time to get there.

A different option to go to the exact location that is used by numerous independent filmmakers is to simulate the location in a nearby region. For instance, let's say that the film contains majority of its scenes set in a small city that could be anyplace, however some scenes are meant to be shot in the city of a foreigner or a popular tourist destination. One option is to locate a location that is within an hour or two which resembles the city or destination. Another option is to purchase footage from a stock source to use for this. In either case, the cost for filming the scene could be reduced.

These are crucial factors to take into consideration when determining your budget, whether you are planning to pitch your production to an agent or make it on your own. If the film contains numerous locations, it may not be feasible on an affordable budget.

4.) 4. What is the top four significant and dramatic scenes from your book?

The majority of books need to be cut to make an appealing film. This means that the less important scenes must either be cut off or compressed to keep interest.

In the example above, there might include scenes in which someone takes a car and parks it to travel somewhere for example;

or perhaps someone travels to the airport only to arrive at a different place. A portion of this travel might be appropriate to make the story more real and place readers within the mindset of the character going to a place. In a film, this kind of shift from one location to the next might not be essential. It is more beneficial to show the subject in one place and then move to another and viewers will conclude that the person travelled to the location by the normal way.

Another instance of cutting can be the time when someone delivers an impressive speech in front of an audience, or gives ideas in an event for journalists. In a book, the speaker could give a full speech, as well as the entire press conference. Films may only include the highlights , and may split between idea to the next with taking pictures of audience reactions.

So, when you examine your book, imagine what filmmakers might and then determine if the book contains enough significant and dramatic scenes that could after being cut as required and edited, be made into film.

5) How important are characters you have in your book?

When the book is transformed into film, the amount of characters will be reduced in the case of a book with numerous characters. If your novel is a complicated story with numerous characters, consider which characters could be eliminated to make the process simpler and reduce costs when making films.

As an example, suppose there's a huge crowd, protest or fight with police in the novel. It could be quite dramatic in the manner it was it is written. But it could not be feasible to film except if some stock footage can be utilized to depict an audience, protest or police act, and then followed by a close-up on the interaction between a couple of people on the screen. For example, perhaps there are a few members of the crowd might engage in the middle of a fight; or the police officer could pursue an angry protester, or there are a few police officers who enter a home to take a suspect into custody.

Consider whether you'll need all the characters you'll be putting in your film because a lot of minor characters could be removed when moving from film to book.

6.) Have you got a dialogue and how is it?

Typically, novels have more dialogue than what you would include in a movie, so anticipate that it will be reduced. The reason for this is that in novels, characters could discuss things, having an argument or engaging in an exchange, which would be normal in the real world. In a film, an extended conversation may become boring, and it is often necessary to reduce it to emphasize the most important aspects.

Another method that often occurs in novels, especially when the story is told from the first person perspective the narrator describes what someone else has said, instead of the dialogue that occurs. In most cases, the writer will say that someone else made a statement. This method can create a less engaging novel, however the screenplay can remedy this issue by turning the statements of who spoke the what in dialogue. If a voice-over narration or character tells the events that occurred to someone else like an interviewer, reporter, or another observer, such statements must be transformed into dialogue within the script.

So, when you think about how your novel could be made into a script the length of dialogue that could be cut out or the way that statements can be made into dialogue.

7.) Are you able to express lots of thoughts or emotions in your book?

In general, if you've got lots of thoughts and emotions, fantasies or flashbacks in your work, it won't make for a great film because the main focus in a film is action and dialogue between characters no matter where the scene is.

If a book contains many emotions and thoughts that need to be communicated through dialogue, through an actor's appearance, body movements, or the character expressing any thoughts directly to himself or herself. The thoughts and emotions assist in enhancing a narrative and convey the character's motivations as well as their intentions and attitude However, they need to be recorded using four primary conventions.

One way to do this is by having an narrator from the first person perspective that introduces the movie, and then makes voice-overs from time the point of commenting on what's happened or what's coming up in the next. A first-person narrator is able to say what he or she thinks or felt during a specific scenario, though you shouldn't use this feature too often or it will become dull or distracting, as it takes the audience away from the story.

Another option is to make the character in the story communicate with the reporter, interviewer or friend, or any other person. Similar to an actor who speaks in voice the character could discuss what been happening, is about to occur, or what they feel about the current situation. This can be done by speaking directly to the interviewer, reporter or any other person or turning the conversation into a narration voiced by a voice.

The third method is to allow the character to explain any thoughts or emotions during a dialogue with characters, like conversing with someone in the family, a friend or therapist.

The fourth option is to have the character reflect on their thoughts by speaking them out loud typically in a soft voice to show that they are thinking, not dialogue.

8.) Have you many fantasies or desires in your work?

It depends on the genre of your book, fantasies or even dreams could be okay. However, if the book is not part of the fantasy genre , or is not about a protagonist struggling with mental health issues or keeping their feet planted in reality A lot of fantasy in a book could slow down a film, or cause confusion to determine what the character is experiencing the world of fantasy or real. A shift to reality and fantasy can work for a book that is aimed at a higher-educational public who enjoys more experimental work, however in the case of a film, this type approach is likely to attract a smaller targeted, more focused audience for films. Similar analysis could be applied to a novel in which characters have many dreams. Certain kinds of dreams, like nightmares, could be suitable for horror films or dreams that have premonitions may be appropriate for suspense thrillers. A film that has an main character who does lots of dreaming could make a film with a dreamy vibe that is hard to sell and distribute.

9.) Do you include numerous flashbacks or shifts in the timeline of your novel?

Another factor in determining whether your book can be made into an effective film is the amount of flashbacks or shifts in time in the film, if there are any. Some flashbacks may be confusing and, when they relate in a different period, the characters and their surroundings must be altered to reflect an earlier time or a setting with a different style for example, old-fashioned automobiles. They can be costly to shoot and you've had to determine whether the viewers are able to follow the repeated changes to the earlier times and returning to present. Perhaps you can manage this by placing dates in the past, and then specify when it's the present to assist the viewer to keep things on track. But certain films make this happen using a different style of the process of filming. So, consider how flashbacks work and how many you'll have to include in your story. Sometimes, flashbacks from the past are not necessary and can be cut off making the book film.

When writing the story being set over a lengthy period of time, different times of the book involve aging an actor or hiring new actors when the characters grow older, which adds more time and expenses for the creation. It is therefore crucial to consider which time periods are essential. In a novel, it might be simple to tell the story through a series of small intervals However, these time shifts could be problematic for the film industry and can get boring to observe the actions of a character every year, instead of focusing on a handful of occasions and then showing how the character's or her story has evolved.

For instance, I was working on the script for a customer that was based on the memoirs of his mother, who went from a baby to a teenager, then an adult, and then changed places between states and cities from one state to the next until she passed away at age 89. Naturally, it could have been a challenge to film considering the million dollars of expenses for various locations at different times that required actors to be in different ages and wearing clothing that was appropriate to the fashions of the day. Also, much of the women's experiences during different periods were not particularly interesting. Therefore it was better to narrow down a few intervals rather than having around 20 changes in time according to the original text.

10.) Does your book serve as an advocacy or message book?

When you've got a cause or message that you would like to highlight through your work, you may definitely use films to convey the message or show the drama of your cause. But , you should be cautious not to make the film preached at or reiterate the message or reference to the cause over and again. A couple of times is sufficient -- maybe early on to establish the viewer's understanding as to the purpose of the film or perhaps at the midpoint to reinforce the message or perhaps at the end to demonstrate at the end that your message is accomplished. In the event that you push your message too much or frequently, you run the risk of becoming boring to the viewer even though you could repeat the message in different scenarios to characters throughout the story. It is certainly possible to have the main character explain their cause when they speak to various people in the story, such as a proponent of changing the course of politics, speaking to different parties and politicians. In a film, after the message has been made clear several times then it is best to ask the main character to state that they are likely to elaborate on something or begin talking about it, and then cut the scene, as viewers already know what the character plans to be saying.

Therefore, if your novel is a powerful message or purpose, you should think about the way it is presented through the movie. If it's shown in the use of action and it can be shown in dialogue for a couple of times, great. However, if you attempt to repeat that in the course of the movie, it does not make for a great film.

11.) Is your novel able to include actual people living or who have an estate that manages their affairs even if they're deceased?

If your work features individuals who are still alive or who have become so famous that their name is controlled by an estate like Elvis Presley, you have to be aware of the possibility of legal actions. The issues you may face may be defamation in the event that you depict the subject with a negative, or incorrect manner, or a famous individual or their estate may have a claim against you due to using their right to publicize without their consent. Be cautious when you decide to film famous people that are living or who have passed away. It is best to consult in with an expert lawyer on what you can and cannot do.

However If your book is based on an historical figure who has died long ago for example, an infamous Viking or Napoleon Bonaparte, you are generally good to go. You can also make modifications in the character they portray, as you're granted creative license. You could, for instance, change Napoleon Bonaparte into a monster who snatches himself from his boat and terrorizes the those in a horror film.

12.) Do the story you have in mind to write have a reasonable cost to allow the film to be produced?

If you've got a compact book that has more than a dozen locations, a couple of principal characters, and maybe some dozen or more secondary characters, an extravagant budget typically isn't a problem. Films can be produced within a few weeks of production, in the course of an additional month or two of prep time prior to production. You must have an achievable budget for an independent production or film.

If your novel has an intricate plot with a lot of locations and characters it is important to realize that it must be reduced to be achievable. As an example, I wrote one novel of 450 pages which had a fantastic story to tell, however there were nearly 4 dozen people, over a dozen locations, as well as scenes that required special effects like a person trapped in an avalanche, and scenes featuring a SWAT team attempting to arrest a suspect and meetings at Federal courthouses. There were also large crowds of protesters, and scenes of raids conducted by police, the FBI as well as the CIA. In the novel, the events were extremely dramatic and written well. But this would be the equivalent of a $30 million production, and is almost certain that it will not be produced in the absence of an existing Hollywood in the first place, and even then it could be too big to make. Therefore, when I wrote the 36 pages of a single-spaced treatise that covered the main plot elements and scenes of this book, which could be made into a series of 10 episodes or a the very costly stand-alone movie, the script was reduced to 9-10 pages of scenes, with some cuts and exposition to include the plot elements which were too expensive to film. After a lot of cutting of characters, scenes along with locations and characters, the story could be produced in an independent film at around 100,000 dollars.

Therefore, you must consider how your book could be reduced or accept the help of an experienced film producer give you this perspective. A more extensive treatment may be needed as a beginning point to define the basic story structure. It is then possible to utilize this treatment as a basis for cutting the film, which is usually not feasible in the event that you attempt to cut these lines in the book. The way to think of it is that the treatment functions as an outline of the landscape, and can be used to plot a course for creating the film. When you first decide the possibility of your book being made into a film you will not have the specifics of the entire film to save and what to be cut, but you'll have an idea regarding what can keep and what you'll need to cut in case you decide to explore the possibility of creating film out of the book.

There you go the most important things to consider when deciding whether your book could be made into film. In the next section I'll present examples of how I've done the book-to-film analysis using these guidelines.

Chapter 14: Example Of Performing An Book To Film Assessment

The first chapter gave an overview of the things to think about when deciding whether and what your book could be made into a movie. In this chapter, I will provide you with an example of how I've evaluated various film projects over the last three years as I've worked on for a variety of companies.

The typical analysis will contain a summary of the book as well as a statement on whether the book could make a great film or not, and the reasons. This is then followed by a summary of the book, though I've cut out the majority of it to keep the confidentiality of the book. If I believe it's a suitable candidate for filming, I'll discuss the process and how it can be accomplished; or, if it's not, I'll discuss the reasons and what needs to be altered in order to make an effective film.

Sometimes, this assessment may be harsh, but it's best to be aware of it early before putting any effort to present the film to an agent or producer, or planning to make the film by yourself that could turn into an expensive mistake. However, If the analysis helps make the necessary adjustments to create a viable script based on the book it could lead to an excellent production.

Even with a novel that's not optimally suited to be made into an film, there's always the chance that a great film can still be made if the scriptwriter is able to make the required cuts and incorporate material making use of the novel as the basis however, he or she can go beyond it to make a film that is inspired or based on it, however with a twist that is different.

Before authors become frustrated by a bad assessment of their film or book and decide to stop, they must realize that an assessment does not necessarily mean that the book isn't good It's just that it might not be suitable without significant changes in order to turn into film. One reason is the fact that films and books tend to be geared towards different types of audiences. For example, a book with a message , or an lengthy discussions about a subject may be extremely well-loved and loved by the people the book is directed by but it may be difficult to convert into a fascinating and successful film. In some instances, the book could be extremely bad, particularly for self-published publications that haven't received the benefit of screen and selection procedure undertaken by an agent or editor. In other instances it's just not appropriate for film.

In that regard, here are the dozen or so assessments I've made for various types of films. The reviews vary from identifying potential for truly great films to describing why the book could become an awful film, and why. In some instances they are of scripts that were crafted by making films, however, the scripts aren't very well-written and require rewriting which is why I have read them as books. These examples were derived from more than three dozen book-to-film reviews I've conducted for various clients.

Review of Books and Scripts with a good chance to become films

Sometimes, if the novel or script has the possibility of becoming film, the critique will provide more information on what changes to make, such as this. I've changed the names to the original script, and removed any specific information and outline about the tale.

I believe that the script has the potential to become film, however I believe the script requires more work and should be structured in either an reading script if the author is pitching their script to a producer , or as a production script after there is a director/producer who has signed on to direct the film. The majority of the suggestions for camera movements are the responsibility of the director/producer , and not part of the reading script.

In a script for reading it is recommended that all of the breakdowns of scenes and characters aren't necessary, but I found the descriptions of characters useful when I couldn't figure out the character or what they did. There were however a handful of characters that weren't mentioned like ....
Additionally, it seems that the first scene

of moving items in ...'s apartment would be a good opportunity to clarify whether the guy is moving into the house as well. The viewer only knows what happens during the dialogue and action and not what the author describes in the description. Therefore, there could be a brief exchange between .... in which he mentions that he has moved into .... 's garage. Another illustration on page. 6 includes the story of the home damaged by the summer that was useless. If this is a crucial element, it ought to be in dialogue so that the audience is informed and not in the narrative that focuses on the action. For instance, ... could declare that the area is dirty because they've not used it in the summer. Another example is to write on page. 9 that they're conducting year-round projects. This isn't something that should be known to the reader unless they mention it.

It is also not essential and distracting from studying the script to write into "Cut in to" at the end of each sequence as it is presumed that this will happen when the situation changes. I found some errors that I noticed, like the use of "sole" in place of "soul." They need to be rectified prior to sending a script in, as some agents and producers are extremely selective. In the movie "Montage," generally these diverse scenes are presented as bullet points written in upper and lower cases, instead of using all caps in the form of a paragraph.

Perhaps as a method to draw the reader's attention into the story, begin by introducing the gunshot that led to ... murdering himself in the process, followed by another old ... recounting the way in which this shocked everyone, and the man wonders why this took place.

In any event the narrative itself is pretty straightforward. SYNOPSIS AVOID

The main drama of the story is in the relationship and conflict between the characters. However, I thought some of the details were missing and could be easily included, as the script is just the 88th page, and feature scripts range from

80-120 pages, and the majority of them are 90-110 pages.

Because the relationship between ... as well .... is the core of the story There should be more explanations of the reason for why this happens. Perhaps there is some tension early on regarding their feelings that this relationship isn't right for them. You could try the same pleading to her parents in order to get them to agree. It's also apparent that the relationship is not happening at a timely pace. We need to see them getting to know each otherbetter, having similar hobbies, and even doing things together.

The mention of ... the driving must be accompanied by a rational explanation. Maybe he needs to solicit his sister's permission to borrow her car to celebrate this celebration.

A second thing you should be cautious about is long-distance conversations that appear to be a speech, such as ... remarks on 19-20. It appears that there could be tensions in this dialogue ... advocates for the relationship, but ... at first is able to come around and eventually comes ... in the end to accept.

I also would like to develop the bond of ... in addition to other things ..., things like taking them to the concert and listening as well as talking about it, and then engaging in other activities together.

... talk about being awestruck by ... way of life, which could be something to cultivate within their group. They could discuss the arts, or other ideas.

Then, some recommendations of around a dozen modifications to consider. Here's sampling:

On page. 28 the mention of the standard uniform, but no air conditioning could be revealed in dialogue and not described in the story. You could also let them wear the uniform during a hot summer day.

In the event on the 24th of p. 24 this may be done to indicate their presence that they are at the party as well as a sign of disapproval from others, that ... as well as ....disregard.

On Page. 43 When you refer to the choir's singing ..., you must include the words they sing.

On page. 53, there's the mention of ... performing great work as a choir leader. Do not just state this however, be able to demonstrate ... that you are the leader of the group and receiving praise in the beginning to hint at future praise. This is crucial when deciding whether to keep him in the job.

If ... will be With ..., it's unclear who .... is and he's not mentioned in the Character list. Perhaps he ....should have appeared earlier before he appears at a special occasion that includes ...

On the page. the 66 page, you do not require camera directions when reading script.

On pages 63 and up there is a inconsistency or confusion with respect to the different years of time being passed and the characters' ages. For instance, if date is 4 years older, ... would be 18 however, he is listed as 17.

It is also important to highlight the growing conflict that is developing between ... as well ... further. In the case of instance, they might dispute over certain things they don't agree on. This could set the scene for them to divorce. In the event of her not being happy and making the decision to divorce comes in a way too quickly.

In conclusion, I believe you've got an excellent idea with an original idea. You'll need to create the script and clean some mistakes and formatting -- or if you require help in this regard, I am able to assist you in this process.

If you are writing the script you are producing it is important to be thinking about the costs of production. As an example, suppose you have various scenes. Each scene will require the setting up of a brand new camera as well as a new crew and camera that adds costs. A lot of these scenes can be reduced, for instance, as low as 30 places.

It is necessary to have a script to establish the cost of production however some production teams will consider what can be changed to reduce the amount of scenes. Consider a range of $60,000-100,000 for this production if it is an independent feature where you make money for yourself.

Review of Books that require more development to make a good Film

Here's an example of the book that has lots of potential, however, the background that was left out of the book was much more intriguing than the story as written. In the end that if more scenes were included that explained the events leading up to the primary crime that is described in the book, the kidnapping which could occur in a variety of ways and could be the basis for a well-made film.

I think that the story ... could have lots of film-making potential in particular since it's is based on real life and includes some dramatic moments. But, I think that there are some details to make an even more compelling story.

The story's basic structure is straightforward forward. SYNOPSIS REMOVED

The story is told through switching from ...'s experience as an abducted person and his family's experience trying to assist and working with local police officers, and a person who has knowledge of the kidnappers. While it is helpful to have three perspectives it is not a complete picture to the events that occur. For instance, ... is in chains, is being shackled, sleeping with restraints Sometimes, the people who are thugs eat, drink alcohol and, at times, give ... food to take in. Even if ... attempts to escape, or makes an attempt to escape, by getting out of the chains, he realises that he isn't able to do it and puts the chains on again to prove that he did not attempt to escape. Then the same sort of interaction with kidnappers goes on.

As dramatic is it sounds, the idea to be kidnapped can be however, it requires more development to build tension and excitement, which is something that could be accomplished when the creation of the script. For instance, there might be additional scenes that deal about ... commercial and the relationship with the person who is responsible for the kidnapping. There may be more interactions among ... as well ..., as the couple .... attempts to establish a business together , and later become an official business partner. There are other possible scenarios of ... creating the kidnappers. There may be an extended scene in which ... can be enticed away from the home to have meal along with ... the person who appears that he is interested in helping in his business. There may be additional scenes ... together with wife to demonstrate the bond they share. It could be a scene featuring other members in the family of his wife that don't agree with ... as well as do not want to contribute to raising the money needed to pay to allow his release. There could be images of the kidnappers interrogated in the police station.

In the end, I think the story has plenty of potential, however it has to be expanded to make it an entire feature. In addition, it requires more suspense and more insight into the various characters.

Review of an Children's Book that Needs to be Expanded in order to be turned into a film or Series

... It is an adorable children's tale about the ... princess of an animal family (a particular kind species of animal) who is obligated to marry someone she does not have a strong connection with, however a shocking thing happens that takes her to a new area where she meets someone she is drawn to.

Synopsis: SYNOPSIS REMOVED

As ... will be the main focus on the book, it would seem like the title would more appropriate to put her name within the name ... as well. .... I would also suggest that the book for children be revised to around 600-1000 words. There's a lot of text and details in the book, considering that it is written to be read by children between 6 and 9 years old. In addition, much of the ideas could be transformed into dialogue and action, for example, having the character .... change positions to show that the self-centeredness of the character as well as ... saying to him she doesn't like himinstead of the writer declaring"that ... isn't an ideal way to express feelings. The story could be changed to reflect this.

In terms of making it animation, believe it has many possibilities and I would like to expand the sections that be more dramatic. For instance, ... could argue with her parents regarding marriage ..., her and may leave. Additionally, they might visit her and convince her to get married. The battle among ... and ... could be extended too. The scene of ... being with .... and his family may be extended. There might be some dialog added. It could be an extended growth of the love among ... as well ... It might be some hinting at ... abruptly changing into a much stronger character or having a discussion on how certain creatures undergo such transformations. It could also appear from nowhere that He suddenly alters his appearance to this form so that it can save her.

To make an independent film the script must be cut down to a minimum. To turn it into a featurefilm, there has to be extra character or plot points. Perhaps the connection between ... with her friend ... can be developed. The plot's additional elements could be discussed, and it could be an hour-long film.

The first tale could become part of a series where it's the first episode. This could be less than a stand-alone feature approximately 30-50 minutes. It seems like this is a great way to go since the following episodes will explore what happens following ... as well as ... wed. Perhaps, his rival ... is plotting to take revenge on him. Perhaps something happens when the kids get older. Perhaps the neighborhood in which they live is a bit difficult or ... aids in overcome these.

If the story is to become part of a larger series, I'd suggest there are five or six more episodes in a limited series or 10-13 episodes for an extended one. A couple of sentences are needed to explain each episode, and the story is presented as a complete series in what's known as an "Show Bible" that has about 10 pages that include an explanation of the series as well as the main character cast, comparisons with other similar series, as well as the very first episode, which is be written as a script based on an existing script book. own.

Another option is to make the princess white, and the prince that woos her in all black. It instantly suggests racial undertones that you weren't planning in the creation of these creatures however, viewers may draw this conclusion. So, it's wise to pick different colors for them for example, creating the princess gold or the prince's purple.

In conclusion, I believe the book has a lot of potential but it has to be developed further into script. Since it's so short it is not necessary to write a treatment in the first place. Instead, scripts can be written in a single step, taking the narrative.

A review of an Script with a Great Proposition, but a poor execution

Although it may help sell books that haven't been able to break out with high sales by putting together and pitching an idea however, a poorly-written script isn't going to help make the book sell at all. Some authors create scripts on their own but they don't do a great job as scriptwriters who are first-time who write too much in the script and leave out crucial information or use the proper formatting that is a sign of an inexperienced. Many people make the mistake of trying to cut costs by hiring a cheap scriptwriter, usually in a different country, where the cost is less. The result is a badly written script. Here's an example that illustrates this problem, with identification information being taken out. The story has a great and original idea for a idea. The basic idea is that (SYNOPSIS removed). Thus, there's a solid base story.

However, the script does have several issues and may need revisions, whether by the writer or a professional writer. One issue is that the script is too rambling, with characters discussing what they are planning to do or about what has been done in the past, and sometimes repeating the same story to various people. Of course, what they're talking about could be converted into actions. Another issue is ..., someone who is going to turn into a key contribution to aiding ... following the couple has separated and he marries her. He is introduced in the early chapters and there's not any indication that he truly likes her or has an ongoing relationship. After the first couple of pages, she goes away throughout the entire script and does not return until the 80th page.

Below is an instance of when the situation could be transformed into action. In lieu from ... discussing the way his friend utilized his vehicle in an armed robbery of an attorney, there might be a scene in the beginning in which he engages in a conversation with a acquaintance ... then informs him that he's reluctant to lend his car. Then, the friend might be the one to commit the theft.

There are formatting issues too. There is no reason to utilize "Cut to" because this is an assumption. There's a lot of unnecessary information in the description of the characters in different ways typically, just their age and a few words about who they are sufficient. This information can be included in the production script however, it is used in a reading script to promote the idea.

There are typos that can be found from time to date, like on the page. 11 within the text ....

There are many scenes in which there is a need to be more established. For instance, what is the reason why ... at the end of the hall for the camera to view ... as well as .... being sexually active. It is important to explained as to the reason why he's walking to the bathroom. As he looks the scene, he could see an extended sequence of two lovers hugging.

Another issue is the transition from a third person narration that is the standard in films to a first-person narrator on the page. 14 and various other points along the way. If there's going to be a narrator on the film, it is set up at the beginning of the film, and then you convert this into a voiceover of a narrator. However, what the narrator is saying is more like an account of the scene than what narration of a narrator actually sounds like.

On the page. 19 of the book, in the event of an exchange of ideas about what supplies to buy, there might be a picture of someone going to the store and taking the items. It is important to show the people who use the items.

There are many more mistakes in the 22nd page ...

If ... is talking about others being jealous I would highlight this, for example, when he ... declares this ... then ... engage in an argument with them. Additionally, you can present ... by demonstrating his talents, and then have the audience comment to express their opinions rather than simply telling the truth about the things they saw. If there's discussion about an article being published in a drama, it can be portrayed instead of having characters debate the topic within the piece. For instance reporters could go to the scene and talk with the principal character or go to a theater and witness ... as well as ... the performance. The reporter then writes about it and you can see the reactions to the characters as well as other people who are reading it. That's why you shouldn't simply tell the story, but demonstrate how the reporter was there and recorded what he saw.

Also, if someone ... speaks about the phone not ringing then have him answer the phone and appear irritated by the calls. In lieu to ... telling you that some people are angry over the issue of. 32, you should show their anger or demonstrate how people call to inform ... the difference. If not, how would ... be aware of this when he's located far away from the incident?

In the same way If there's an argument that ... has been in a coma for 3 months, don't declare that. Take him to a fight before he goes into the hospital.

In the simplest way, go through the script, and make sure you correct any mistakes, eliminate any extra descriptions about the characters, and turn many of the conversations about events into action and let the character's wife take on an active role in the script in order to set up ... for her to marry her.

A Book Review with more potential as a series

Sometimes, a novel is more suitable for the form of a series rather than just an individual film, especially when it follows the lives of characters through different periods of time and has multiple characters. In this scenario an episode could focus on an alternate stage in the life of the individual as demonstrated by the review below.

... offers great potential as a film about a teenager who is placed with an adult guardian following the death of his parents, creating conflicts over the access to his money as the boy continues his studies and gets a job. It feels like it could be an episodic series that has several episodes, each of which is the different stages of his life, and not being one film. In addition, the way it is it is written, each section of the novel lends itself to a distinct episode.

The book is well-written with a variety of scenes and dialogues, which allows it to be turned into a movie, instead of having a lot of thoughts and emotions that are appropriate for novels, but need to be either eliminated or converted into dialogue or narration with voiceovers. In this instance there is a lot of dialogue in a lot of scenes, but it's possible to condense the dialogue to make clear the primary idea. The series of films typically last from 30 to 90 minutes. An 80-90 minute film can be made into an independent film, as well as being a film within the series. This is my recommendation for the very first film in the series. Therefore, my focus is on the latter.

In the first story SYNOPSIS was removed from the first story.

Due to the way that the story is written , with clear scenes and dialog for each of these experiences that the protagonist ... encounters It is easily adaptable as a coming-of-age tale. It's ideal to stand in a single film or episode focusing on this -- instead of trying to incorporate the different events the character ... have. Additionally, the script could utilize foreshadowing in order to briefly introduce an additional persona ..., who is likely to develop into a love interest once they get older.

And then, the second chapter of the novel, that leads to a different episode in the series ... He is at high school. There, begins to form relationships that lead to employment as a waiter, and then is the target of a scuffle. The details of the story are removed.

In the following part, he ,... is a student at college and is involved in a romantically growing affair with ..., and, again, this leads to a new episode that follows. The next episodes when he's at graduate school and when he is married, and later divorces ....

In short it is a novel which has a lot of potential to be made into a film, but it's best to promote the book as a series with the first installment able to be part of the overall series or stand-alone film that marks the beginning of the three or four-part series.

Review of a Book That requires more action to be Transformed into a film

The problem with turning certain novels into films is that there is a lack of action , but a lot of reflections on the past, ideas about what the characters should take on in the future as well as an account of what the character experiences while engaging in various things. In some cases, characters think about what an individual is thinking and feeling and how they might respond or create a relationship. These musings could be great to be included in a book because they offer an knowledge of one's beliefs to values, beliefs, and their place throughout the globe. However, they aren't a good fit for a film, as it relies on visual and dialogue to convey a story. If the action in the book could be extended for film, it might work. This review highlights this point.

I believe ... could become a movie however it'll require some time before it can be transformed into an action-packed story that has dialogue that goes beyond the writer's reflections on the events in her past relationships shaped her present perceptions and feelings, so she can build a stronger relationships with her partner in the future. Even the description of the story seems a bit unclear, considering that this story could be about any story about having bad relationships and looking for the best one, and there's nothing to draw in potential viewers.

To be made into film, the novel must have a full narrative even if it's an emulation of events from the past. These stories must contain dialogue and settings. These elements can be added to the creating the scripts by the screenwriter or author however, at the moment the basic plot structure is not included in the book. However, I went through about 150 pages, and then skimmed through the remainder until the end. There are instances of triggers however, they are only briefly mentioned, and not events with characters and locations which can easily be turned into scripts.

Although the book is written chronologically, starting in May 2014 and ending in December, this reflective style continues throughout the entire book. it's difficult to figure away the essential events that cause these reflections. In a film, these other plot elements need to be added or developed. The central idea of the narrative is that love can be extremely difficult and it is possible to not make the best decisions. However, for a film we require the experiences of certain relationships between lovers to bring the story life. The viewers must see and feel what it takes to make a love-hate relationship, not to be informed that a hate relationship occurs when one is in love with someone but eventually fails to work since love is an endless cycle of seeing around and round. It what appears to be the main concept of the book, even though there are also reflections on different issues that arise within a relationship.

Although there is a lack of story, this could be created into a script from this, either by using my imagination to develop the story arc , or by soliciting input from the writer about the kind of incidents that should be included.

What is the first thing that comes to mind when thinking of the fundamental structure of the story is a woman writing in her journal. And when she is writing some thoughts on what been going on in her relationship, she can find a way to connect to the events. These do not have to be presented in chronological sequence if the film is made into collage or montage where thoughts on your relationship can be followed up by the events related to relationships the author has had that have occurred in the past. Some of the events that could be formulated in response to the thoughts and feelings of these individuals could be:

An initial meeting which individuals are attracted to one another;

Certain experiences can demonstrate a growing affection for nature, like walks along the beach or in the woods visiting an amusement park and then squeezing close on a ride

Certain incidents illustrate the tension that arises from differing opinions that lead to open conflict moments when he steps away angry, and times when she leaves angrily but they come back together

A marriage that has kids, and lots of changes and obstacles in the marriage. taking care of the kids and the children feel ripped because of the fights between husband and wife as well as their love for each other when they get together;

A divorce can lead to uncertainty on both sides over the best way to break apart or go on due to the fluctuating nature of the relationship.

There are some controversies on both sides that create tension within the marriage in addition to the fluctuations in the marriage;

A time of healing following the divorce. This may involve trips to romantic destinations to let one forget

A new relationship develops, and fears getting into the same situation previously in relationships.

Also, the comments on the script, which can go on for around a year, can serve as an ideal frame for the story. As the woman writes, she will be able to recall certain events in the past, which make the comments more vivid and turn into something that could be captured. This method is similar to the method used to the story in The Marriage Story, where the narration of the story is conducted by a character who discusses the events that are happening to the characters and the review leads to an event that took place during the course of time. Another instance of this method is Gone Girl, where the protagonist is played by Ben Affleck is trying to consider what could have occurred in the relationship that caused the girl to abandon her.

With this further development the book can be transformed into a thoughtful and sensitive tale, however, it will require the inclusion of actual events with dialogue as well as fleshed-out characters to allow this to happen. They could be designed by the author , or the author could provide some insight into the actual events that inspired her ideas. The treatment could be used to outline various thoughts on relationships within the book, with a sentence or two on the kind of incident to be remembered. A script that is between 90 and 120 pages might be written once the treatment has been accepted. Because there is only a brief narrative in the book it is a good candidate for the idea of a stand-alone movie rather than an episodic series, which requires more intricate plots and a variety of characters to support the lengthier form.

A Film Review that could be Of Limited Appeal and More Suited to a niche Market

A film may be interesting in its storyline, well-acted action scenes, interesting characters, and even a unique subject.

However, it may not be a suitable film-to-book project due to the fact that it isn't appealing to the general public and it could be difficult to locate an uninvolved producer. If the author is able to raise funds, the book can be developed into a movie. A good example of this is a movie which it could appear to be Christian film because it is based on numerous Christian characters and imagery but is in reality an anti-Christian critique which is evident in my review of the book.

... It is an art form of spiritual parable in which angels are tasked with protecting humankind and fight against demons to protect souls of humans. At first glance, the novel appears to have an appeal for those in the Christian marketplace as a family movie and at first, it appears to have a TV show or film series potential , with numerous stories based on the struggle for human souls. There are diverse characters who require protection and various obstacles facing the main characters or angels who are fighting other souls. However, a deeper analysis of the book exposes the author's goal to shake up Christian believers and leaders with criticism of their faith in the manner the story closes with main characters engaged in sinful actions and angels defeated. Maybe if the characters who were in the story found a way to be saved and decided for a more godly existence and live a godly life, the film could be successful and be successful within the Christian market. If the film concludes with a failure to live the Christian faith and the writer would like to use this film to propagate the gospel message, it is unlikely to be a successful sell to producers. It might be even more difficult to release should the director get the funding and create the film.

If anything, and with the possibility of a different outcome to the plot, it could be a fascinating film built on its own unique story. The story starts - SYNOPSIS removed.

The story could be easily made into a film. the differences between people and the spiritual beings could be addressed by combining animation and real-time action to the spirits. If the film concluded in the central character becoming a convert to Christianity after all the trials The film would be successful on the Christian market. However, once it concludes in the middle of the story with the character renouncing Christianity in order to avoid the temptations offered by Satan and Satan, the film ceases to convey a positive messages about faith that draw in Christians. Instead, it will trigger their angerand being uninterested in watching the film.

A Book Review which may have a strong appeal Based on current events if It is further developed

Sometimes a film made from the book may have huge potential due to the fact that it addresses contemporary issues that are relevant, but the film may require additional research to be made. In this situation one of the main considerations is whether a film which is current today will be relevant in two yearstime, which is how long it typically takes to go from developing a script to a completed film, and then finding an appropriate distributor. The distributor will require an additional six months to acquire all the necessary deliverables for the distribution of the film to retailers who will stream the filmand and offer it as a Video-on Demand nine (VOD) product or, in certain cases, organize theatrical screenings. On the other hand certain books about pivotal contemporary events might have a an appeal for the long term because they've been a significant influence on society , or tell an engaging story that has a long-lasting appeal, such as relationship with a loved one, a family crises, the friendship betrayal or a battle in the face of the elements.

This is an example of story that tackles the current major issue -- the emotions of anger and inequity that are fueling this Black Lives Matter Movement, that is expected to be a lasting influence on the society over the next few years. If the movement does not decline however, the film will be a hit, as it's about a significant issue within American history. The book could require further work to make into a film, if it requires a more compelling story or a more developed characters. A skilled scriptwriter can assist in helping build the book in order to create an engaging film. Additionally, if it appears that a book could be suitable for film then a sizzle reel could make it more noticeable when pitching it. This is the method I advocated in this article about the book that has a lot of film possibilities.

... It seems to be a great candidate for both film and promotion because it concerns an Black immigrants to America. United States, given the rise of and the Black Lives Matter protests. This has resulted in increased curiosity in films and books which deal on Black Americans and racial issues.

The plot is straightforward, with an affair and business issues as well as a court proceeding and making decisions on how to proceed and where the best direction to take.. SYNOPSIS REMOTE.

However, the novel requires some work to transform it into a film that is successful. The narrative as it stands is often a bit confusing due to the change between the third and first person for characters. Typically, when there is one who is narrator from the first person perspective this person will remain exactly the same throughout the story. Therefore, it can be confusing to change to a different narration midway through the story. However, this could be resolved by changing the story into scripts, as the focus is on dialog and action. In this case, one narration by a single story and any thoughts expressed by others could be expressed in the form of the character speaking out loud, but generally, such thoughts can be transformed into dialogue. Likewise, emotions are expressed through the facial expressions of the actor.

Another idea that could be considered when transforming this into a movie is to include additional drama. As an example, there might be the possibility that a certain family member is going to object to the event, but to add more drama, there's a disagreement with the family member until he changes his mind. Additionally, there could be more said about the protagonist's involvement in a number of criminal acts to accomplish his objectives or goals, and there could be an argument where he attempts to hide what he's committed.

However the script can focus on scenes that have more drama, like .... It's also better to begin the script by ... receiving an email requesting you to complete a task for example, like travelling to another country to meet to discuss the relationship with the woman from the country where he was raised up.

In the end I'd suggest turning this into a feature film because I believe this is extremely appropriate in light of current the current events. To achieve this the film would require the synopsis and script to be around 80-120 pages, typically 90-100 pages in the present. It is possible that the characters could have different experiences, like their time in America. United States. If they have problems in their country of origin, the it could be part of a series in which the script is presented as an episode of the show in a Show Bible. It's like the book proposal however, it is for pitching the idea of a TV or film. Another suggestion is to make an introductory reel that could be used as an ad for the book as well as a script trailer. It will help promote the book as well as increase sales. Additionally, it could draw more attention for the story from agents and producers.

Review of a Book which is Too Theoretical, Preachy and a bit confusing to make an Excellent Film

Sometimes, a novel may not be a good fit for the form of a film when it's excessively theoretical and abstract as well as preachy or unclear in regards to the identities or the character. In these situations it is possible that the book needs to be developed so that it could become a different story, which means it may not be worth the effort to make the story work. It may be more beneficial to use what you've discovered about what makes the best film and create the future book with potential of film in the back of one's mind.

This was what I experienced when reading the next book, which focused on the struggle for souls. The book was written by an firmly Christian tradition. The ultimate goal was to shield souls of the souls from the evil forces. However, in this instance the book had several flaws that resulted in making the book film something that may not be a good idea. The fundamental outline that the text follows in broad terms.

... tells the story of a fight for souls led by a girl who is young after family members have been hurt or appear dead as a result of acts of the spirit being and his assistants. SYNOPSIS REMOTE.

It is not clear what this girl or her family members are since it is initially believed that they are an indigenous American farm family living in the Wild West. Perhaps the battle is going on against spirits in a mysterious location, possibly in the realm of spirit. But , at the end of the day maybe the battle is taking place in the present or perhaps in the park or in the back of the church, and today people have access to modern technology, for instance cellphones. Yet, at present we don't know the location of this battle.

There are scenes in which there is a disagreement, like the possibility that certain characters might decide to leave God to join forces with the evil forces, and whether they'll be rewarded or executed for disloyal behaviour, most of the battle is lengthy dialogue that is more like a sequence of speeches than conversations. A lot of this discussions are very philosophical, looking at the relationship between loyalty, commitment as well as truth and integrity are among the aspects affect one's choice for joining God or the evil one in his quest to win the fight for souls.

Another issue is that characters are stereotypes or depictions of various spiritual forces, which means it's difficult to connect with or feel for any of them.

The lengthy discussions on spiritual principles are a contributing factor to the lack of connection to the plot, and this is true both when the forces of evil fight to save the souls of people or when there is a rift within the groups.

There is also some confusion over the exact location and time this war of souls is taking place. As of the conclusion of the novel it appears to be taking place today in a park where certain characters are using mobile phones, but the soul battle appears to have taken place earlier in time or even on a higher level.

Furthermore the text itself is quite short. And after the lengthy philosophical discussions are cut short and the book is also too short to be made into one of the feature films or an episode of the form of a film series. It's because film is an image-based medium that is driven by actions. As previously mentioned there's a lot of dialogue and the majority that is composed in the form of a speech regarding what the protagonist is going to perform or about threats regarding what might happen if another character fails to do something. The kind of conversation could be appropriate for a novel or a novel, but the moments from a conversation or lengthy speech of a character could be used in films, for instance cutting out the lines that are the key the main. However, lengthy speeches or discussions can become boring when they are incorporated into films. They could be used in various dramas with a theatrical element, however, they aren't effective in the film.

Another issue is that a lot of speeches are not just excessively long, but also are overly preachy , with messages that are repeated over and over. It is acceptable to convey an important message, but it should be integrated into the story and the action while the message is repeated repeatedly in lengthy bits of dialogue, which are repeated back and again.

If the dialogue was reduced and the other issues addressed that can be accomplished when writing a script to the story, it'd be too small to be a feature which typically runs between 90 and 120 minutes. It's also too small for an episode of an ongoing film series, as the typical length is 30 to 90 minutes with the majority of episodes running between 45-60 minutes. The entire story, if condensed, will likely be around 20 minutes, which means it's not enough for commercial films.

In the event that these concerns can be addressed, then the potential market for this film could include the Christian market that is a huge market for movies. This film may be a success in the event that the writer makes these changes and provide an explanation of why the characters are targeted. It could, for instance, be a tale of the members of the family and how they participate within the local church and why they make them an ideal victim of the demon and the evil forces that he symbolizes. The writer could then decide if there's enough information to write script. After this, he might write a logline and summary of the story as well as an introductory reel before attempting to pitch the story for film.

Review of a book that Could be an Film or the basis for a Series

Sometimes the information in a book can be good enough to be made into a single film , or be made into a series, based on the amount of material taken of the original script. This can be especially relevant when the novel is written as a personal memoir or a compilation of events to be used in documentaries. The question should be addressed by considering marketing aspects, and the script could be designed to accomplish both, based on what the prospective agent or producer wants to look at -- a logline as well as one script for a separate file and the Show Bible and sample script for the show.

This is the case with this memoir, filled with the highlights from the life of a famous person who was once admired through an individual from the family. I've altered the names in this review to show.

... It is an intriguing autobiography of ... from his spouse, who composed the book shortly after his death. He started his career just upon his death ..., and, after some initial struggles, he became extremely successful, and gained international recognition and became a part of numerous businesses.

The story starts at the time that ... the two ... the first came into contact.

The main focus of the book is on the high points of the last two decades during which ... stood at the height of his profession, and it's filled with photographs of the many occasions he attended as well as others famous people he had the privilege of meeting. While the main focus lies on ...'s memories or reactions details about famous people he had the pleasure of meeting.

The book starts with ...'s the early years before the beginning of his career but it's mostly about his work as well as the individuals he worked with as well as worked with. SYNOPSIS removed.

The book has a great possibility of becoming an actual film or a series depending on how it's constructed. Given the number of descriptions in the book of events as well as the stories associated with them, the film has to be able to provide a common voice to connect the various stories, and it is best to arrange all the events described in the book chronologically. Maybe an opening could include ... in the highest point of his fame before returning in time to where it all began. Maybe the wife of his or someone who represents her could provide that unifying voice. They could also present the story via the use of narration over voice or the interview of a reporter or a TV host. If the script is developed, based on how the script is created the novel could be made into a standalone film that runs between 90 and 120 minutes, or it could be presented as an episodic series that features different parts from ...'s life starting from the initial days of his career, to the highlights of the following two decades. The final episode could feature the final years of his life after he ... was laid off after pursuing a new career and made large investments that have had varying outcomes.

There are many options for making this book into series or film scripts can show the way to develop. To in promoting the book and the script, a two-minute sizzle reel could be created with a narrative about the film's appeal , using photographs from the collection to demonstrate ...'s the film's life. If it's an individual film, it should have an overview and a logline. If the film was became a series or a series, the Show Bible might be developed to help pitch this. Perhaps there is an independent film that can also be presented as an episode of the series. The method to determine the best approach depends on how much the story will concentrate the story of ...'s the career of the actor or the stories of other people who that they have met that can be incorporated into the idea of a sequence of stories. The most effective approach could be determined during the process of creating the script by evaluating what is the most effective way of presenting this information. In addition, due to what the issue is matter, it may be necessary to include video and images when they are accessible from various sources. If they're in good health, the documentary could include interviews with those who work in his field, to share their experiences with him throughout the time throughout his lifetime.

Review of a Book that has Possibilities. Possibilities with a Small Market due to the subject

Another factor to consider when determining whether a novel can be successful in its transformation into a film is the market. Many authors dream of creating a highly acclaimed Hollywood production that is a hit with millions of people; they dream of their novel becoming an instant blockbuster. While all things can be done in an industry that is uncertain, in which even executives and producers who have long careers may not always know what will work well or fail however, many books are unlikely to be made into an entertainment film with a mainstream appeal due to their subject matter. Instead, they could appropriately be independent low-budget films targeted at a specific market, for instance in the case of a film inspired by a unique or sexually taboo subject. This was the case with the next book that could have great potential, but in the confines of a smaller market for independent films.

.... is a good idea to become an independent film, however, due to the subject matter it is likely to need to be an independently production. It could attract the attention of a project similar to The Tiger King, which has an interesting group of people with strange sexual relationships , accompanied by murder, accusations of animal abuse, murder and much more, even though the show was able to be viewed because of the sheer insanity of the incidents.

The book also takes you inside an unorthodox religious sect with a sinister leader who inseminates women within his community, faints regarding it and then forces the man ... in an engagement with an unidentified woman with a variety of issues. It appears that the majority of the congregation members are suffering from issues of their own. This is the kind of tale that's sure to draw an interest that is morbid similar to The Tiger King. Although the author is keen to go with real names, it may be better to choose fake names until the story is reviewed by an attorney prior to when the author presents the story before any producers. After that, a producer could decide to go with real or fake names. There's too much chance for defamation lawsuits and a film production company would not wish to take on that risk.

However, the book, no matter if it's a novel or memoir is well-read. The story is told by vivid images that would be ideal for a film. There are a few tangents that include discussions about religious sects, a visit to a foreign location as well as some bizarre rituals. They could be eliminated from the film since they are a sudden end to the narrative. If they are included, they can be conveyed quickly.

In all cases the story's basic premise is
SYNOPSIS REMOTE

The story can be adapted to any film idea and is able to be made relatively cheaply because of the limited places like rural roads, the interiors of a home or office, church and even a funeral. Being limited in locations is a factor in making it affordable for it is an indie film. I would recommend it as an alternative film which may be viewed by a wide audience, like Tiger King, and the next step is to write an overview and treatment and then, in the best case, an outline and a short film with images that will aid in making an introductory pitch for the story be noticed.

Review of the Book in a Unique Space with Expositions that are too long Exposition

In certain cases the books that are set in a different time and location have too much detail, which means that it appears more like an anthropological study of a different culture, rather than an engaging story taking place in the. A book like this could be well-suited to being transformed into a film when the story is more dramatic created by either the writer or the scriptwriter, which can be seen in the book that follows.

I believe this ... is an intriguing and unique premise as well as an interesting storyline. However, to make this motion picture, the screenplay requires more plot and less explanation. While writing the script I'm able to add it in the areas that appear to be lacking.

I think that the fundamental idea of having a single character ... to be an observer and narrator all of this is intriguing, however I believe it could be enhanced through a voice chat to ... that is our main protagonist for the majority of the story but after he travels to an alternate planet, another character is introduced as a central character ... whom is first introduced when he was a young child 12 years old, and later as an adult around 50. Maybe the main character could be introduced earlier and some of his growth ... the character and their education could be halted to allow for the object that is said to possess supernatural powers, but it will only reveal an ability that all humans possess in their minds or in their souls.

In all likelihood there is a chance that the initial section may be cut down or condensed for the film to the point that ... is given his task. The story indicates the idea that ... exists living in the society that is built on conformity and lack of empathy however, he is a different person by having different opinions. There is a possibility that more can be made of his development into adulthood in that we might witness ... fighting the rules that hold him from being more expressive. It is possible that he will be drawn to a different member of the community. I believe the story requires some drama at the beginning, not only an account of what the surroundings are like. It's similar to sitting in a lecture hall as the environment is described by lecturers who describe the habits and customs ... in ... along with about a dozen students.

Instead of sitting watching, ... could demonstrate his rebellion by leaving class to go out and enjoy flowers or bucking the rules. Afterwards, the teacher will bring him back in the norm. Some of the best parts from the class could be portrayed in a more detailed manner, however, the lengthy description of the new society in these lectures will not make sense in a film where story, drama and the visuals used to tell the story are essential. There may be cutaways during the lecture however it is important to focus a film on one main character, or perhaps two or three characters or even a small group of characters, as in a heist movie. However, even when there are several primary characters, generally the first three characters make an impact. In this case, the main character doesn't show up until later in the story, and at first the character is only listening to the talk.

A few of the introductions about the setting could be brief by explaining that this all happened thousand of years ago. Then, the explanation on souls and spirits might be better be explained by the way the character ... is transported to another world to learn about their belief system and magic. Also, the discussion of spirit nature at the beginning should be included in the process of ... looking to fulfill his purpose instead of providing this information via lengthy discussions and exposition that are difficult to produce visually and dramatic for film. When creating your script, these concepts can be briefly discussed in order to establish the frame that tells the story. However, it's crucial to focus on the main story.

There could be more details on the way in which ... was a rebel He can also discover some of the best aspects in the new environment at the school. However, from page 31 to the 97th page, much of the text reads as lectures. Perhaps some interactions ... in conversation with fellow students or even the professor could be included here.

There's a statement that ... experienced many experiences in rising up his ranks in this particular society from another planet. However, instead of saying that it will occur, it's more beneficial to let him go to these places. If he studies the past of the region that he's currently living in it could be a good opportunity to explain the things he discovers about the world around him. Perhaps a cutaway would illustrate what he observes instead of hearing the details of what it's like in that particular world from page 121 through page 140. There's a lot of telling and it requires to be told by some means.

Perhaps instead of discussing the ways that native people have created myths and legends that help to overcome their fears and anxieties on the page. 176 the story could be made into a dramatic film by having the indigenous people participate in an event. Also, there needs to be not just more story or action in the novel to make the story into a captivating film, but also more dialogue. I would also include the quest of an object ... earlier because the hunt for the object is a major goal for the main character. I would also make the search for it more exciting.

In conclusion, I believe the core idea of the novel is sound, however it is in need of being changed into a script that includes more action, drama and character development in order to captivate the audience. The best way to begin is with a treatment that will highlight the key elements of the story that need to be written into the script, and then the dialogue can be added in later. The treatment could include further scenes that can extend the story. Even though the story was set hundreds of years ago, it feels like a science-fiction or fantasy film, both of which are popular genres that aid in selling the film.

Review of a Book based on Real Events with the Names of Real People

Sometimes, a novel draws upon real events and employs the name of actual people, which could cause problems when making films. In a book, the authors are more free to use actual events and names which are based on an editorial or literary licenses, but when it comes to films, there may be legal obstacles to overcome which include the right to publicity as well as accusations of defamation. Therefore, it's better to consider changing names or claiming the film was an inspiration, or speak with a lawyer, in addition to taking into consideration the normal considerations to make a book film. This is an instance of a novel that did not just require further development, but also brought up legal issues.

I believe ... could be an interesting idea for a movie or book however, it has to be further developed. At present, it reads more of an outline, and makes for boring reading, as it mostly is a narrative, with only a few exceptions, like the final story, in which there is a personal story of what transpired to ... that was the inspiration behind the book.

Although it's interesting to make use of the last names as a reference point to describe their crimes, there's no obvious connection between the five men , apart from their names. In addition, as there could be legal concerns in making use of the names ***** and implying that he has committed certain crimes, even though this isn't a case that can be decided at an investigation, it may be better to alter names of ..., as well as the others who have identical names.

There are a number of ways to make this either a book or film.

Let me first discuss the possibility of a book. I believe that the book can be created if you expand on the information provided to make the cases become more vivid, such as by putting the reader on the situation while the case is being examined, for instance from the viewpoint of a journalist following the investigation. The book can be made into an "as as based on" or "as inspired by" story that focuses on the various cases, and then include additional details of what transpired. For instance there was a lot of coverage in the national press about that ... instance which could be used to fill more specifics. I'm assuming that these other cases may contain articles about them as well. If you want to dramatize the case it is possible to use these articles as information. These details will help you when writing an outline for a film, although you might need to alter details for legal reasons.

I also suggest starting with your own story because it's very personal and dramatic, and has was the inspiration for other stories. With the possibility of allegations of defamation, defamation and privacy invasion and your safety in the event that the person is as dangerous as you claim it could be a valid reason to alter the name for at least a while until a lawyer is able to examine your manuscript to the producer or the publisher and advise with actual names or not. At first, it is best to make use of a pseudonym until everything is being sorted.

You can then use your experience to develop an outline of the things you saw. Following the account of your experience, you'll be able to write about the other instances and each becomes a element of the work and the chapters within each section can be used to tell the story in a more compelling way.

This method can be discussed in a proposal if are in search of an traditional publisher, as well as adding two to three chapters to total 40-60 pages. If you're self-publishing and want to finish the publication.

If you're planning to make film, you must make an Show Bible featuring each of these stories as an episode, and then make use of sizzle reels (a script trailer, which functions similar to an ad for a book) to advertise the script and help the film stand out. The film could take one direction.

1.) The film may be presented as a documentary. It could include actual footage of interviews with suspects neighbors, prisoners or anyone else who is willing to share their stories with you, as well as reconstructions made by actors. Then, every story within the series could be told in three or four episodes. One example could be The Innocent Files, Unsolved Mysteries as well as other crime tales that use this strategy although it could be more expensive and time-consuming to employ this method of documentary. If you read the Show Bible, you would detail how you'd do this. The story might include either you or an actor who is you. The film may begin with you speaking to a reporter about the way the incident affected you and the information you discovered concerning your neighbour .... which led you to believe that he was the culprit, then an reenactment of the incident (though I would suggest changing the names for this). In the form of a Show Bible, you describe every episode in one or two sentences that led you to suspect the person, then write an extended script for the way each story will unfold.

2.) The film may be viewed as a collection of stories that are fictional and based on authentic stories. This is what I would recommend since it's cheaper, more efficient and more straightforward as a documentary and usually a dramatic venture that is based on actual events has the potential to be more appealing to viewers than a documentary straight. In this instance I'd also suggest beginning with your personal case as well, where the person who represents you might be able to speak with anyone to relay your story. This person may be a reporter, a friend or counselor, lawyer or a government official that you'd like to take action. The stories that you've written down can be told with 3 or 4 episodes, and maybe you could tie the stories through the narration of a voice actor and conclude each episode by setting the scene for the following story. Perhaps you can imagine a connection between these men, which was discovered through the investigation of the case in question -- maybe they have distant relatives or had a relationship, or even had a business in common. The final episode could include an analysis of the weaknesses of the criminal justice system, or the unanticipated linking of people or some other thing. The show bible is the Show Bible to describe the series, and also include the script of one episode, which is approximately 30-90 minutes or 30 pages and each page is equal to one minute.

In conclusion, I believe this project is a good idea, but it needs to be written as either a script or book, or both, including samples of chapters to be used in the proposal, as well as a complete script for a single episode, as well as an official book trailer for the series. If it is an actual documentary or a dramatization inspired by a real-life story, the story needs to be told through scenes and dialogue. And to pitch, you could make a sizzle reel of both the film and the book as this will help to attract agents, editors, and film producers to go through the script or book and become excited about the idea.

Review of a Book that has Great Potential, but too Many Details that Must be trimmed

The issue with turning documents into movies is that they contain too much information which needs to be cut. Often, the memoir of someone who is extremely successful is more like a lengthy resume instead of an inspiring story of fighting against odds to achieve success. The story of overcoming odds is a recurrently appealing kind of film, similar to the survival of disasters tale is because people are drawn to seeing the struggling character break through and achieve success. However, too much reiteration of success after success is a tedious task and should be drastically cut back so that the film can perform well. A review of success could include in final few scenes of the film. It could also be mentioned in the credits on the side. Sometimes, authors might resist this cutting since they perceive that film to be a tribute to the amazing accomplishments they've made as a proof of what they have become. However, to make a captivating film, these credits must be able to emphasize the significant changes or events which led to the success. A more comprehensive list of accomplishments could be added to an additional slide or two prior to the credits.

The following example is an account of a life that could be an excellent film, but requires some drastic editing in order to allow it to be successful. I've removed identifying information and have written a few paragraphs to make it less specific.

I believe ... is a film that has the potential to be made into film, however it will need to attention to certain crucial events to bring out the drama as well as the concept about discrimination it ... faces and wants to draw the attention of in order improve the situation.

One of the major advantages of it is it's well-written and is simple to follow along as the author relates different events in his life. It begins in his early years of living in poverty in a different country. He then describes receiving aid to move to America to study at the top universities, before becoming professor, and eventually achieving huge success in the field. The author has certainly accomplished well and won numerous awards and praise throughout his career. He also talks about the occasional issues he faced in the past when he was able to stand up to certain officials from his country of origin academic, business, and academia and also meets with the representatives of various activist organizations.

For an upcoming film, many of these particulars must be removed, like the experiences of students learning for and passing several tests. It is important to highlight the events that are likely to can be the most appealing to the audience. It is acceptable to record them in a chronological manner or perhaps with the voiceover of an author, or in a story that is told to an important person in the life of the author. In addition, some of the routine activities like going to classes, having discussions with professors to discuss exams, and so on could be presented as an montage of footage of various events and the narration of the event through a voice-over, what transpired during a specific time period.

In addition, certain occasions that are of more general appeal to the public could be included, while other events like regular meetings with academics and industry, could include in the montage, or excluded, since films typically range from 80 to 120 pages or more often 90-100 pages in the present.

For instance, the link with ..., which they eventually got an engagement may be emphasised. It is possible to highlight how they got together and how he was enthralled by watching her engage with her in activities outside of school. There may be videos about how he learned the trade with his father. A few of the most interesting experiences from childhood can be included too however, a lot of details regarding preparing an academic program could be streamlined. It's also fascinating to draw attention to the political and historical background in the country of birth as the author grows up however, the specifics concerning obtaining a scholarship or the funds needed to attend top American colleges may be streamlined.

In light of this mix of dramatic events as well as specific descriptions of educational processes, meetings, and discussions of the grading process I would suggest creating an essay that highlights the events to be featured within the movie. In order to do this, I'd look over the draft and develop an description of what happened that will be highlighted. Then, it would be used to develop the script. It will include dialogue. There is a lot of dialogue in the descriptions of various events. this could be added to the script, based on details of what transpired and the people who acted in what position. The discussion of different scientific methods could be demonstrated through experiments and discussions in the laboratory. Certain details are too complex for a typical public. Instead, a discussion about the things that scientists are currently working on could be a good way to present something similar, but without the need for explanations and names of scientific research. Also, the work of companies that conduct research could be handled in a similar manner to emphasize the most important and compelling.

In conclusion, I believe it could work as an film if reduced to focus on what is most intriguing and exciting for the general public. This can be done by writing a first treatment and then using it to guide creating the script. To draw attention to both the book as well as the script, I would suggest creating a three-minute sizzle reel, which is similar to the trailer for a film or book. Additionally, I suggest creating brief synopses of about 1-2 pages as agents and producers often request it prior to viewing the script. The title of the book is long and also contains some unfamiliar words to describe what the writer is, therefore the film requires a and more appealing title.

Summarising

These examples show that certain books are able to become great films however, their appeal could be a broad movie that is able to attract large audiences to those that appeal to a narrower segment of the population. In many instances, the potential to be a successful film is based on removing unnecessary details or expanding the story by adding other events or either. In some instances, because there is so much to develop the book might not be a good film unless the writer would like to make significant adjustments and maybe even write a sequel in the light of the elements that make a great film.

When you have a clear idea of what is necessary to transform your book a film, it's important to develop the necessary materials that will assist you when pitching your film agents and producers or taking steps to create the film on your own. Although a synopsis and logline or perhaps sizzle reels, may suffice to present the film rights of an upcoming book, selling the rights to film doesn't usually work for self-published books or a book with high sales and/or the author is a an established platform that has a large following. However, for the majority of books, it is necessary to include additional materials in accordance with whether the book should be created as a stand-alone movie or as a series of films. It is necessary to provide a logline, synopsis as well as a the script for a stand-alone movie or an Show Bible and script for an episode in the series. Additionally, a sizzle reel may aid in both cases to make your work be noticed and draw an interest in making an original film based on your novel.

So, evaluating its potential for a book the initial step to determine whether it is feasible to make the book film and then determine the actions to follow. If the book has potential, but it is possible to make modifications and preparing the necessary materials to promote it and then the initial review of the book will help determine what to do next. Think about this review as the decision of whether you want to go on an excursion or not. If the signals are favorable to take the trip then you can determine the best route on your trip.

This is what I'll explain following. The process of creating a treatment acts as an outline of the kinds of scenes are required to be included in the script and in the film. After that, I'll go over how to create a synopsis and logline. The logline should be a concise and compelling description of what the movie is about, in roughly 15-25 words. The synopsis is a half page, a page or a 1 1/2 page explanation of the main moments that take place within the movie.

Conclusion

Making a screenplay that is successful isn't easy. It's a long-term commitment and requires time, effort and practice to develop their skills in the field. But, the standards of Hollywood for the most successful films won't be changing, and there are tools that can assist you in doing the best job you can. You can use formulas as well as structure that we've covered in this book to help you.

With all the tools available to help you build your foundation, it's your responsibility as a writer to provide a fresh style and voice to Hollywood. The audience will never get tired of new content or a classic story told with a fresh viewpoint. Make sure you do what you have to be doing to stimulate your imagination. maintain a healthy lifestyle and surround yourself by things that stimulate you.

In time you'll notice that regardless of whether you're writing your first screenplay, the second, or the your tenth screenplay, you'll return to the formulas that we've mentioned in the previous paragraphs. You've done an excellent job of of acquiring the industry's knowledge and abilities that you'll eventually master.

Consider these components as a recipe that you'll refine as time passes. It's a recipe is being perfected but you'll discover that certain situations necessitate you to spend longer in one section in comparison to the other. Perhaps for certain stories, developing characters will be easy, and for others working on the main character's goals is more difficult.

Whatever the hurdles are you in the way, or even when you are tempted to quit and giving up, do not succumb. Keep a notebook close by always, so that you can write down ideas, thoughts, words, and thoughts that come into play. As creative people individual, we are never sure what the most brilliant ideas will strike us. It could happen during your morning cup of coffee, or while you're enjoying a meal or listening to music or perhaps watching a film. It's possible to get inspiration from people you encounter during your day-to-day activities and then weave them into a fresh story to create your screenplay. Screenwriting is a continuous process. Make a commitment to a schedule of writing and allow yourself plenty of time and space each day to dedicate yourself to your writing. The process of becoming a screenwriter is slow, so don't get too hard on yourself if you're not getting the immediate reaction you've been hoping for. Keep your focus on your story because you'll eventually get there.

Hollywood is a challenging market, but you can make it if you follow the suggestions I've laid out for you. These are the most reliable methods for how to succeed in this competitive industry. The journey that awaits you, as the writer is now officially underway. There's no way for you to go back down and there's no better time to get started on developing your skills than now, today. Thank you for purchasing this book. I'm looking forward to watching your screenplay at the big screen in the near future!

www.ingramcontent.com/pod-product-compliance
Lightning Source LLC
Chambersburg PA
CBHW071842080526
44589CB00012B/1085